31 Small Steps to Organize Your Paper

a dhucks small steps book by
Shawndra Holmberg, CPO-CD®

Copyright © 2017 Shawndra Holmberg

All rights reserved. This book or any portion thereof may not be reproduced or used in any manner whatsoever without the express written permission of the author except for the use of brief quotations in a book review, blog or article, with attribution to author and book title.

Although the author and publisher have made every effort to ensure that the information in this book was correct at press time, the author and publisher do not assume and hereby disclaim any liability to any party for any loss, damage, or disruption caused by errors or omissions, whether such errors or omissions result from negligence, accident, or any other cause. References are provided for informational purposes only. Readers should be aware that the websites listed in this book may change. The author may recommend certain products and services. The author has no financial relationship with these companies.

ISBN-10:154073188X

ISBN-13:978-1540731883

Cover art copyright © 2017 Shawndra Holmberg

other books by shawndra holmberg

31 Small Steps to Organize Your Life
31 Small Steps to Organize for Weight Loss

online courses by shawndra holmberg

31 Small Steps to Organize Your Paper
www.hyh.thinkific.com/courses/31-small-steps-to-organize-your-paper

Table of Contents

what did you say this book was about?...................................1

what's the best way to take these small steps? 2

past, future, or present?...3

5 reasons you struggle with paper 4

start at the end 6

use a timer...7

ready to take that first step? 9

Step #1 Make your space more attractive 10

Step #2 Make the time more engaging 13

Step #3 Make a home for your mail...............................16

Step #4 Get off the mailing list 18

Step #5 Make a home for your magazines.....................21

Step #6 Divide and Conquer..24

Step #7 Unsubscribe from catalogs 27

Step #8 Unsubscribe from magazines 29

Step #9 Commit to stopping the flow of emails 31

Step #10 Create a mobile processing center..................35

Step #11 Choose an initial paper storage unit................37

Step #12 Build in maintenance......................................39

Step #13 To Shred or Not to Shred................................42

Step #14 Keep or Toss? Create guidelines 46

Step #15 Start at the end..49

Step #16 Set aside a specific day...................................51

Step #17 Test your paper maintenance system 53

 Step #18 Go paperless — carefully................................55

Step #19 Get your first 'Take Action' tool ready............58

Step #20 Get your second 'Take Action' tool ready........62

Step #21 Get your filing tools together 66

Step #22 Ready — Set — SORT 70

Step #23 Take Action 76

Step #24 File it 81

Step #25 TBR — To Be Revisited 85

Step #26 Prevention — Refuse 87

Step #27 Prevention — Reduce 89

Step #28 Prevention — Reuse 92

Step #29 Prevention — Recycle 94

Step #30 Final Storage Unit 96

Step #31 Keep Going 98

Step #32 Thank Someone 101

Appendix A — Glossary 103

Appendix B — Shopping List 112

Appendix C — Organizing Zones 114

Appendix D — Special Categories 116

Appendix E — Resources 119

so, who's this shawndra person, anyway? 121

and what's this about a dhuck? 123

what did you say this book was about?

Stop sweeping your piles of paper into the nearest box minutes before company comes. With as little as 15 minutes of action a day and applying the next 31 steps, you'll begin to breathe easier knowing that you'll find what you need when you need it. These 31 Small Steps will have you conquering your mountains of paper so that next April you'll be able to hand your tax accountant a more organized file, on-time, without that wild, destructive sweep through your office. You'll build maintenance into your system rather than put it off, which will encourage you to discard old documents in manageable chunks instead of ending up with boxes of paper to toss and shred. No more late fees because you misplaced your bills; your papers will have a home.

This book contains small actions, thoughts, ideas, and strategies that will move you towards controlling your flow of paper. It's just thirty-one simple ideas that you can take one at a time. Thirty-one small steps towards getting your paper dhucks in a row. Taking one step a day over the next 31 days will not be enough time to get through years of accumulated paper, but you'll have the tools and the systems to begin digging out from under the piles. You'll begin to lose the paper piles and regain your life and space.

what's the best way to take these small steps?

The doors we open and close each day decide the lives we live.

Flora Whittemore

Well, that's kind of up to you. It's your book! But I think the best way to go about it is one step at a time, one chapter each day. Don't read them all in one sitting without taking action.

The steps are written in order to help you build on previous steps. Could you pick a step at random and work on it? Yes, but you'll find that key tools were created in previous steps. So, if you want to journey through this book randomly, you may need to jump to a previous step. The whole point of taking these 31 Small Steps is to keep things simple and to minimize the overwhelm. Whatever approach you choose, pick one idea each day and take that small step!

If there is a step that doesn't make sense to you, or it isn't in the order you want, or you just don't feel like doing it — mark it for review later and move on. Don't stop. Don't toss out the rest of the steps. Don't struggle. Mark it and move on. Keep going.

Set a timer for 15 minutes to help you stay focused and on task. You could set your timer for 25 minutes or 10 minutes, whatever works for you. When the timer goes off, check in and confirm that you're working toward the goal of that step or session. You could then start the timer again or stop for the day. Either way, give yourself a high five for taking action and making progress.

After each step, I've added a section for your notes, scribbles, or doodles. You also have a wide margin for note taking. Highlight sections, quotes, or ideas you want to check out again. If the thought of writing in the book is horrifying, think of this as a workbook. You're supposed to write your answers and ideas in it. If, after writing notes in each section, you find that you must have a book free of marks, send your marked-up book to me at Shawndra Holmberg, 140 Shockey Lane, Building F, PMB# 110, Butler, PA 16001, and I'll send you a new book. Email me at simplify@dhucks.com to let me know it's coming and to make sure the mailing address is still current.

past, future, or present?

You may be holding onto paper because you're not willing to let go of the good memories and feelings associated with it. There are better ways of recalling those memories than holding onto paper that is causing you stress.

If you're holding on to paper because you're not willing to face the bad feelings or memories that the paper brings up, I'd suggest letting the painful papers go so you can move on.

If you're keeping paper because of the good or the bad feelings, you're in the Past.

If you're keeping paper because *someday, maybe* you'll need it or want it, or because you think someone else might want it, you're in the Future.

If you want to live and find joy in the Present, then your paper needs to reflect that. The paper you keep needs to be for the present, for *your* present.

It's your choice. Do you want to be stuck in the Past, waiting for the Future, or enjoying the Present?

The secret of health for mind and body is not to mourn for the past, worry about the future, or anticipate troubles, but to live in the present moment wisely and earnestly.

The Teachings of Buddha
    Bukkyo Dendo Kyokai

5 reasons you struggle with paper

> *Organizing is what you do before you do something, so that when you do it, it is not all mixed up.*
>
> A. A. Milne

#5 - You don't know what to do with it. You're not sure if you should keep it.

You need knowledge. You will need to learn the purpose of the various papers and why it may be important to keep them. In Step #14 I've given you some resources that will help you establish your guidelines for keeping.

#4 - You expect you can do more, have more, and read more than is possible.

You need realistic expectations for the time you have, the space you have, and the energy you have. If you find yourself saying "I might need this *someday*" dig deeper and determine when *someday* will be and what the circumstances are that makes *someday* likely. Explain this out loud to yourself, a non-judgmental friend, or a professional. Then decide what's realistic for you and create a paperwork system that fits. This book is intended to help you set realistic expectations.

#3 - You either have a system that is too complex or you don't have any system at all.

You need a workable system. A system includes the tools you need to organize, process, and access your papers when you need them. It also includes the strategies you use to keep up to date on your bills, file the papers you need to reference again, and properly dispose of those items you don't need. If your system is too complicated and takes up too much of your time, you'll begin to let things slide and put off doing your paperwork. If you haven't established a system at all, then you won't know what to keep or where to keep it. This book is all about building a workable system for you.

#2 - You feel overwhelmed and don't know where to start, so you give up.

You need to start. And you can start small. This book is titled *31 Small Steps to Organize Your Paper* because these steps are doable. You will walk through establishing your paper strategies, setting up a workable system, making choices and determining guidelines. You'll move from one decision to the next, and I'll be there to help you with every step. This book will help you start to move out of overwhelm.

#1 - You put off doing your paperwork because you'd rather be doing...anything else.

You need to take action. You will need to put time into getting your paperwork done. I understand that there are numerous ways you can spend your time that you consider more fun or exciting. The goal of organizing your paper and routinely processing the incoming paper is not to have organized papers, but to free up your time and your thoughts to enjoy your space and create the life you want. Manage your paperwork better and you can stop wasting your time worrying about the paper mountains and feeling bad about the procrastination.

start at the end

It is good to have an end to journey toward; but it is the journey that matters, in the end.

Ursula K. Le Guin

How much time are you willing to put into **maintaining** the paper once you get it cleared?

_____

Is that daily, weekly, or monthly?

_____

Make an initial estimate now of how much time you are willing to put into **maintaining** your paperwork. We will revisit this idea again in Step #15, but for now, how much time do you think it will take you to manage your paper? How many minutes or hours? And is that daily, weekly or monthly? You can think of this as admin or administrative time.

Your decision can be changed at any time if you find that you want to do more or do less. This is just a starting point that you'll use to evaluate your paper strategies and systems. If you don't want to put in the needed time, you'll have to simplify. Keep in mind, quickly accessing your papers and the information is a goal, but your ultimate goal is probably enjoying more free time, achieving your dreams, and living your purpose. Your system needs to support that, not take away from it.

Now that you have established an initial limit on how much time you're willing to spend maintaining your system, this becomes the baseline amount of time to devote to sorting, deciding, and organizing your paper. Yes, you will need to put in extra time as you're going through your papers and information and setting up your systems and creating your strategies. However, on those days or weeks that life has other things for you to do, you can limit your efforts to your minimum paper processing time and continue to experience progress. Next, look at the weeks ahead. When will you be able to add in extra time (in 15-, 30-, or 60-minute increments) to implement these 31 Small Steps to get your papers and information under control? Will you put them on your schedule now?

If you're like many individuals, you're willing to put it on your schedule, but you also push that commitment aside when anything else comes up. Would you be willing to establish an accountability partnership with a friend, supportive group, or professional (organizer, coach, or therapist)? Often we don't keep appointments and commitments to ourselves unless we've committed to someone else. If you want to join the Dhucks' Paperwork Party™ and commit to us, please go to www.dhucks.com/paperwork-party.

use a timer

Throughout these 31 Small Steps, I'll suggest that you set a timer. You can use the clock on your phone, an app, a kitchen timer or a special timer like Time Timer® that makes time visible. The goal is to use the timer in small blocks of time to keep you focused on the task at hand. You'll break your administration or paperwork time into doable chunks. And you'll be able to tell yourself that you only have to do it for a set time. You'll be setting limits to the time you spend managing your paper. It's not about spending your life dealing with your papers. It's about setting aside time to take action so the papers don't overwhelm your life.

I recommend Time Timer® for clients as it provides a visual cue of time passing with its red wheel around the screen as time counts down. You can choose a blue, green or yellow wheel if you prefer.

I'll often ask you to set your timer for 15 minutes, but the actual block of time is your choice. It could be 20 minutes, or 30 minutes, or 23 minutes. The goal is to break down the hour or two you've set aside to make progress with your papers into smaller chunks of time. After 15 minutes (or your chosen block of time) the timer goes off to remind you to get back on task if you've wandered down memory lane, to take a break if you're feeling tired, or to encourage you to take on another 15 minutes because you've got the energy to continue.

I also have found with clients that setting a timer gives them permission to quit working on their paperwork after fifteen minutes or an hour and fifteen minutes. They stop dreading the paper maintenance because it no longer has to take their whole day.

Never give up on a dream just because of the length of time it will take to accomplish it. The time will pass anyway.

H. Jackson Brown, Jr.

ready to take that first step?

(It won't bite. Dhucks don't have teeth!)

Don't wait until everything is just right. It will never be perfect. There will always be challenges, obstacles and less than perfect conditions. So what. Get started now. With each step you take, you will grow stronger and stronger, more and more skilled, more and more self-confident and more and more successful.

Mark Victor Hansen

Make your space more attractive

It's likely you don't find sorting, filing, or acting on your papers as exciting (or as fun) as the other activities in your life. This is one reason you delay doing it. The first step is to make your paper processing space more engaging, attractive, interesting, productive and maybe even fun.

Every accomplishment starts with the decision to try.

Gail Devers

Make your space more attractive. Since you will spend time with your paper in this space, make sure that the area is enjoyable and conducive to reading, writing, and deciding.

Increase the lighting in the area. Set up task lighting by using a table or floor lamp next to your area. Open the curtains and add natural light to the mix during the daytime. During the evening hours, close the curtains to keep the light inside and make it cozy.

Add a plant or some flowers. Hang an attractive picture or a funky piece of art. Bring in a splash of your favorite color to the area. Give your space color, warmth, and beauty, even if there's more to clear and declutter.

Add movement to your paper sorting. Spend some of your sorting time standing if you can. A kitchen counter, a table, or a dresser can be used as a temporary sorting area when you need a taller workspace. You'll find that the freedom to move your body gives you freedom to let go.

Engage all your senses: sight, sound, taste, smell, touch/movement.

Turn on the music. Working to your favorite dance music will rev up your energy and keep you moving forward. You'll feel your progress pick up. Or put on a comforting beat to keep your paper beast calm and quiet.

Bring in aromas and smells. You could use a comforting scent like lavender or patchouli. Increase your energy and focus with peppermint or citrus. Whether it's your personal fragrance, a candle (careful around the paper), or a diffuser, engaging all your senses while handling your paperwork will enhance your experience and effectiveness.

Finish by clearing your workspace. Before you leave the area, pack up any unsorted papers and put them back in the box or pile they came from. Stop 15-minutes early and finish your filing, tossing, scheduling, and mailing. Leave your area ready for the next session, even if you think you'll only be gone for a couple of hours. How many times have you intended to return to a task only to be sidetracked by life? Spend time at the end to create a space you want to come back to.

Keep your paper processing area clear between sessions. Don't create new piles. Don't drop anything in your work area, even if you think it will be "just for now." If your processing area is only a quarter of the dining room table, a small desk in your spare room, or the couch in the living room — keep it clear between sessions. A cleared workspace should attract you, not your stuff.

Do a little victory dance every time you see your space clear and free of clutter.

Increase lighting

Bring in color, texture or nature

Stand up while sorting

Move to the beat

Spice it up with your favorite scent

Clear your space before you leave

Keep your space clear between

SUMMARY

Tools: Varies. Keep it simple. The goal is not to decorate your space but to add an item or two to make your paper processing environment more attractive and productive for you.

- A timer

Time Estimate: 15 to 60 minutes. Moving a lamp to your paper area could take less than 15 minutes. Adding an attractive touch could take an hour. Save 15 minutes at the end of your organizing session to clear your space, put your tools away, and stage the paper for another day.

Add Notes Here ⬊

Make the time more engaging

One reason you may put off getting your paperwork done is that you think you have to do it alone. You may feel that paperwork is a solo effort, a solitary experience, and that you have to sit apart from others. Do you save your paperwork for times when others are having fun or relaxing? That seems unfair. But you don't have to be by yourself while you're processing your paperwork.

Friendship is born at the moment when one person says to another, 'What! You too? I thought I was the only one.'

C.S. Lewis

If you have kids, consider doing your paperwork when they're doing their homework. If you decide you have to make dinner while they're working on homework, consider enlisting them to help with dinner. It will save you time, build their cooking skills, increase family time, and everyone could then focus on paper and homework.

Consider experimenting to see if you're more productive at a busy coffee shop. I've had several clients happily focus on completing reports or handling mail in the midst of the activity a local coffee shop provides. They just needed the stimulus of noise and movement to concentrate. Others need a much quieter environment, such as a library. Keep in mind that not all paperwork can be done in public due to the lack of privacy and security. But it might be just the thing to get you started.

You can also make paperwork more social by asking a friend to sit with you as you sort, process, and organize your papers. Make sure your friend knows the rules — sitting, no talking or offering suggestions, and definitely no judgment. Maybe they could bring their papers and do their paperwork, too! A win-win for everyone.

A professional organizer can be a great body double (a term organizers use for being present with a client while the client clears, sorts, or processes). Professional organizers can help you stay focused while you work, keep you out of overwhelm, and offer guidance on setting up a system that will work for you. A professional organizer who specializes in working with individuals challenged by chronic disorganization can offer targeted solutions for you. You can find these organizers through the Institute for Challenging Disorganization (ICD, www.challengingdisorganization.org). Another great organization that can help you find an organizer is the National Association of Professional Organizers (NAPO, www.napo.net) though not every organizer in NAPO specializes in chronic disorganization.

How will you make your paper processing time more engaging?

_____

You can make your paperwork a social event and add an accountability partner by joining a clutter support group in your area or my online Paperwork Party™. These paperwork parties are scheduled throughout the month for individuals who need and want to make progress on their piles and keep their paperwork maintained and under control. Participants join via a video call to stay focused, receive encouragement, and learn answers to their vexing paper questions. Since these sessions are virtual, you can be where your paper is and still make paperwork a more social affair. For more information on the Paperwork Party™ go to www.dhucks.com/paperwork-party.

SUMMARY

Tools: Varies with your social solution.

- A phone if you need to call a friend
- A computer to find an organizer
- Join a group or sign up for a Paperwork Party™
- A bag to take your papers with you if you go out
- A timer

Time Estimate: Making it social shouldn't add more time to your paperwork; it should increase your productivity. Though finding your body double, chatting with a friend, travel, and getting settled will take time, once you have a routine down, there's no extra time involved.

Make it social

Share the load with your family

Take your work out for the day

Be accountable:
- Ask a friend
- Hire an organizer
- Join a group

Add Notes Here ↘

Make a home for your mail

Mail comes in almost daily, and it needs a home. Get a basket or box that is big enough to hold one of the large mail envelopes. But don't make it so big that it becomes a dumping ground for everything. Choose a container that will attract your attention — your favorite color or a beautiful pattern. If the container has a lid, don't use it. Lifting the lid will slow you down, and it's a flat surface that may tempt you to drop the mail on top instead of inside the box. Think of this basket or box as a target. Your goal is to get the incoming mail to this drop zone every day. This is your **Mail Home**.

Rather than buying a container at this point, look around at re-purposing a basket or box you already have. Try it out to see what you need. Learn what works and what doesn't.

Take another 15 minutes to round up any stray mail you find lying around. If there's more mail than your box can hold, grab another box as a temporary holding container until you get caught up on processing your mail.

Place your new **Mail Home** where the mail is most likely to come in and be dropped. Placement will be an experiment. You're looking for the best spot that will increase the likelihood that you'll drop the mail there. You can place the container near the door where you first come in. You can put it where you drop your keys or your purse/bag/briefcase. Speaking of which, do they have a home? Or you can put the mail basket in the kitchen if you routinely bring the mail in with the groceries and such. As I mentioned, this will be an experiment because you need to find an easy target location, but you don't want it to become a dumping ground for stray items. You'll want the home to be big enough to hold larger envelopes, but you don't want it to be so big that it takes up too much space or holds too much mail. It isn't always as simple as you think it should be. Try and try again until you find a place and a container that work for you.

...the great thing in this world is not so much where we stand, as in what direction we are moving.

Oliver Wendell Holmes Sr.

Find the best target zone for your mail.

Today your goal is to make a home for the mail. You may have rounded up a little or a lot of mail. The rest of these 31 Small Steps will help you create systems, strategies, and habits that will make processing your mail easier.

SUMMARY

Tools:

- An open-topped box or basket
- A timer

Time Estimate: 15 minutes or less to find your container for the mail. 15 minutes to round up the mail. As you find mail in other places, drop it in its new home.

Add Notes Here ⬊

> Create a "home" for your mail
>
> Try different locations for your drop zone
>
> Build the habit of dropping the mail on target

Get off the mailing list

> *I am only one, but still I am one. I cannot do everything, but still I can do something; and because I cannot do everything, I will not refuse to do something that I can do.*
>
> Helen Keller

Stop the flow of unsolicited mail from companies seeking new customers and pre-screened credit offers. It's called junk mail for a reason and getting off the direct marketing mailing lists can save time, money, and the environment.

Sign up at www.dmachoice.org to set your preferences on receiving catalogs, magazine offers, and other mail offers from companies who are looking for new customers. Most companies buy their mailing lists from Data & Marketing Association (DMA) and agree to abide by the preferences you set. You can either stop all unsolicited mail or pick and choose the items you want to keep. It can take from 30 to 90 days for your choices to take effect. The DMA opt-out is effective for five years.

It's quick and easy to register on-line as a new user, read the main paragraph, and chose to be removed from all categories. It will take you longer if you want to pick and choose what to stop or allow. I recommend that you stop all categories for now. When you're done with these 31 Small Steps you can go back and turn on the ones you want.

You can mail in your request, but it will take longer and you still have to be able to access the Internet to get the form. You'll also pay $1 to have your request processed manually. It's much easier to register and choose on-line, so ask for help if you need it.

Reduce the number of pre-screened credit offers you receive in the mail by registering at www.optoutprescreen.com. You will also be directed to the site by DMAchoice.org if you choose to unsubscribe to "Credit Offers" in the "Manage My Mail" section.

The pre-screened credit offer opt-out is effective for five years from the date you make it. If you want to permanently opt-out, you can choose the Permanent Opt-Out by Mail option and complete the electronic opt-out process. Once that's completed you will be able to print, fill-in, and mail the "Permanent Opt-Out Election" form.

Registering to be removed from these mailing lists does not stop all unsolicited offers. The companies that you've already done business with have you on their customer list. You will need to contact the company directly and ask to be removed. Each year, you'll get a letter explaining a company's privacy policy. Use the letter as a reminder to update your mail preferences with that company.

Getting off the mailing lists and dramatically decreasing pre-screened credit offers is also an important step in protecting your identity and finances from thieves. The less junk mail with your personal and financial information on it, the fewer opportunities for it to fall into the wrong hands.

> Protect your identity and finances by opting-out of the pre-screened credit offers.

Junk mail is only a part of the stream of paper that flows into your home. Steps #7 and #8 will help you with the catalogs and magazines.

Place a reminder in your calendar to opt-out on junk mail and pre-screened credit offers again in five years. If you use a paper calendar, use a sticky note at the back of the calendar. Move it into the new calendar each year.

Register & opt-out at dmachoice.org

Register & opt-out at optoutprescreen.com

SUMMARY

Tools:

- Your computer
- A timer

Time Estimate: 10 minutes (or less) to register on-line as a new user with dmachoice.org and choose to be removed from all categories. It will take longer if you pick and choose what keeps coming. Another 10 minutes or less with optoutpreseen.com. If you mail in your requests, plan for 30 minutes or more to download, print out, and fill in each form.

Add Notes Here ⬊

Make a home for your magazines (catalogs, too)

Today's goal is to create a home for the magazines, catalogs newspapers and other reading material you choose to keep until you've read it. This **Magazine Home** is not for storing print material you've read and want to keep for archival reasons. You're building a drop zone for your reading material so that you know where it is when you want to read it. Yes, you will sort and let go, but that's for tomorrow.

Every choice moves us closer to or farther away from something. Where are your choices taking your life?

Eric Allenbaugh

But before you even touch the first catalog, magazine or newspaper, establish your guidelines for keeping it.

Set Your Guidelines

Catalogs: Consider letting all the catalogs go. The companies will send you a new one soon unless you unsubscribe (Step #8). Decide now about what you will do with a new catalog. Yes, you'll drop it in its home, which you'll create in a moment. But how long will you keep it? Why will you keep it? Why do you need it? Does it support your goal of getting your papers under control? Write your answers in Add Notes Here section on the next page or in the margin.

What purpose is that catalog serving?
_____

Magazines & Newspapers: Use the Rule of 6 to form your guidelines. If the magazine is a monthly, the information is old after 6 months. If it's a weekly, don't keep it longer than 6 weeks. A daily newspaper is old after 6 days. Let the magazine or newspaper go if 6 more editions have been published. If the Rule of 6 doesn't work for you, what will? How long will you keep an edition? Will you let it go once you've read it, or will you hold on to it for six months (or weeks or days)? Write your answers in Add Notes Here section on the next page or in the margin.

What is your magazine retention policy?
_____

If your goal is to collect and hold onto all your magazines for the future possibility that someone might find your old magazines invaluable, you'll need to decide whether you prefer to live in the present or the future (see Past, Future, or Present on page 3).

Establish a Home

Choose a box or basket to use as your home for magazines. This home can be your target zone for holding all magazines, newspapers, and other reading material. You could keep your catalogs here also or grab a second box for your catalogs. Place this **Magazine Home** near where you read or in a convenient location to grab and read. If you created two homes (one for reading material and one for catalogs), place each home where you will be most likely to look at the information.

Keep the home small enough that you can read all the material in a month. Make the time to read or let it go. Once you clean out your magazines and organize them (Step #6), you don't want to get bogged down by unread piles again. The goal is not to store your magazines but to read them and then let them go. Use the container as a visual reminder to clear out the old and make room for the new. Once the magazines and material reach the top of the container, it's time to apply your guidelines again.

Take 15 minutes to round up any magazines, catalogs, newspapers, and other reading material you find lying around. If there's more than your **Magazine Home** can hold, grab another box as a temporary holding container. You'll sort the stack tomorrow (Step #6).

Set a Read-by Date

Will you commit to setting a read-by date?

_____

Any magazines, brochures, newspapers, or articles that you keep longer than your magazine retention rule must have a read-by date attached. Write the date you commit to reading the material by on a sticky note or directly on the cover; during the next clean-out session if you haven't read it, toss it. This goes for books also. Honestly, if you have a stack of to-read books, how many of those books have been there for over a year? Over five years? Give it another six months, but if you haven't read it by then, let it go. You probably were reading other books in the meantime. Don't wait for *someday when you have time*. Open up your space to living (and reading) today.

Step #5 to Organize Your Paper | 23

SUMMARY

Tools:

- A basket or container for each home
- A pen or marker
- A notepad, journal or this book to record your magazine and catalog guidelines
- Sticky notes for the read-by dates
- A timer

Time Estimate: 30 - 45 minutes: 5 - 15 minutes to set your guidelines; 10 - 15 minutes to find the new home for your magazines; and 15 minutes to round up your magazines and catalogs. Set a timer for 15 minutes for each of the three stages (guideline creation, finding your new **Magazine Home**, and rounding up the reading material). No stopping to read. If you find that setting the guidelines is bogging you down, talk it over with a friend or maybe even a professional (organizer, therapist, or online magazine reseller).

> Establish your magazine retention policy
>
> Create a "home" for your magazines and other reading material
>
> Gather the reading material
>
> Set a read-by date

Add Notes Here ↘

Divide and Conquer

When faced with a decision, choose the path that feeds your soul.

Dorothy Mendoza Row

You now have a home for the magazines, catalogs, newspapers, and other reading material (Step #5). Today you get to choose what stays until you've read it and what goes. Grab the guidelines you established and the reading material you collected in Step #5 and let's begin sorting.

Divide the magazines and catalogs into three categories: keep, unsubscribe, and let go.

Keep

The keep pile will go back into the **Magazine Home** and **Catalog Home** (if you have one) for you to read. Use your guidelines to determine which ones stay. In addition to setting a read-by date on this material, decide when you'll set aside the time to read it. If you see yourself as a reader, then read. Make the time to read the magazines you bring into your life and space. Stop waiting to get to it someday. Get to it now, or let it go. Your time is too precious to waste on *someday* piles.

Unsubscribe

This pile will include magazine and catalog subscriptions that you don't want cluttering up your space anymore. You may have magazines you enjoy, but if you don't have the time to read them all, consider unsubscribing. Make these magazines a treat you give yourself by buying one copy to read over your favorite beverage at a local coffee shop. Or grab one edition to take with you on vacation.

Put a sticky note on these magazines and catalogs, write "unsubscribe." Place these either in your **Mail Home** or in your **Magazine Home**. Anywhere that you can easily grab them in Steps #7 and #8 to unsubscribe.

Let Go

These are magazines and catalogs that don't meet your guidelines to keep, are no longer of interest, or no longer support your goals. The let go pile will be recycled, thrown away or donated. Let's start with donating.

Come up with a list of locations that might accept magazines. Your library might want recent editions. "Recent" usually means less than six months old for most magazines, but call to check. Your doctor's or dentist's office might be interested in last month's edition, but when will you go? Senior centers and Veterans Affairs centers may be happy to have older reading material. Call to find out. Share your magazines with others if you can. Schedule it and do it this week. Get the magazines out of your space.

If there's no group or location that will take the magazines, they need to go into recycle or trash. Yes, I give you permission to put it in the trash. Sometimes it takes so much effort for you to recycle that you put off doing it. I care for the world, and you do too, but you won't be able to save the world if you're drowning in paper. Once you've cleared your space and are no longer buried in old reading material, then focus on recycling where you can.

If you're spending time looking through the magazines for articles you want to read, toss the magazine in the Keep pile with a read-by date. Today's goal is to get your stack sorted.

> Don't hold onto the past. You'll find more things that interest you tomorrow. Make the space now.

Review your magazine retention policy (Rule of 6)

Sort into **Keep**, **Unsubscribe** & **Let Go**

Determine read-by date for the keepers

Unsubscribe comes in Steps #7 & #8

Let go by donating, recycling or throwing away.

SUMMARY

Tools:

- Sticky notes
- A pen or marker
- Trash bags for trash
- A bag or box for recycle
- A container for the donations
- Your calendar to schedule the donation drop off or call to confirm that they'll take the magazines
- A timer

Time Estimate: 30 - 45 minutes. Set a timer and sort in 15-minute chunks of time. Fifteen-minute blocks will keep you focused on sorting rather than reading. Save the last 15 minutes to take out the trash and recycle. Another 15 minutes if you need to make phone calls about the magazines. If you don't have curbside recycling, then that and the donation drop will take longer. If you can't get them to their new home today, put it on your schedule this week and get them out of the space. Get it out sooner rather than later.

Add Notes Here ↘

Unsubscribe from catalogs

You established a home and organized your catalogs earlier in Steps #5 and #6. Now you'll begin to unsubscribe to catalogs. Pull out the catalogs you marked to unsubscribe and let's begin.

I walk slowly, but I never walk backward.

Abraham Lincoln

Start with www.CatalogChoice.org to pick and choose the catalogs to stop. You can also request to stop delivery of phone books in your area through CatalogChoice.

Grab a few of the catalogs and opt-out now. You may have more catalogs to stop than you have time for today. If so, pick a day next week to return to this step and unsubscribe to another handful of catalogs. As the catalogs come in, opt-out immediately or mark the catalogs and put them in your **Mail Home** for later processing.

Once you've registered, you can read the main paragraph and chose to be removed from all categories. It will take much longer if you want to pick and choose what to stop or allow. I recommend that you stop all categories for now. When you're done with these 31 Small Steps, you can go back and turn on the ones you want.

Getting off the mailing lists and dramatically decreasing unrequested catalogs is an important step in protecting the environment and your local landfills. CatalogChoice estimates that their opt-out services have saved nearly a million trees, prevented over 1.4 million pounds of trash going into the landfills, and conserved almost one million gallons of water.

If you feel you have to keep some catalogs, be picky about the ones you keep. Choose carefully. Not all catalogs support your personal goals. If your goal is to decrease your shopping, then saying 'no' to the catalog is easier than saying 'no' to a particular item. If you want to continue receiving a catalog, set some guidelines about how long you will keep it before it needs to go.

Remember to put the catalogs you choose to keep in their home box or basket so that you know where to find them when you want one.

SUMMARY

Tools:

- Your computer
- A timer

Register & opt-out at CatalogChoice.org

Time Estimate: It can take 15 minutes or less to register on-line as a new user and opt-out of all catalogs. If you want to pick individual catalogs and adverts, give yourself 5 minutes for each catalog.

Add Notes Here ⬊

Unsubscribe from magazines

If magazines and newspapers are filling up your home faster than you can read them, unsubscribe. Don't focus on the information you haven't read or the money you've paid, concentrate on the space and time and guilt you'll save. How much time are you actually spending on reading them? If they go unread, unsubscribe.

Not what we have, but what we enjoy, constitutes our abundance.

Epicurus

Pull out the magazines you marked to unsubscribe from their home basket or the **Mail Home** and let's begin to stop the flow.

Start with ones you can check out at your local library or ones that you no longer find interesting. It's likely that your interests have changed. By decreasing the amount of information you allow to enter your home and life, you can focus on reading what does come in. Unsubscribe from at least one magazine today.

You may have to search a bit to find the phone number or website to unsubscribe, but it will be worth it. The cancellation information is often on the same page as the publisher and editor information. You may also be asked for a subscriber number from the mailing label.

Commit to saying NO to renewing subscriptions. Identify which ones you want to renew and which ones you don't. For now, you could put this list in your **Mail Home** or with your bill-paying tools. Once you create your mobile mail processing center in Step #10, you can keep it there.

Though this step is about unsubscribing, add an ounce of prevention — commit to saying NO to free subscriptions. It will save you from unsubscribing later.

Even after you've called or gone on-line to stop your subscription you may get another edition or two. It takes time. If you don't renew, they'll still send you several more editions with reminders to renew. Stay strong. Sending the mailing label and a letter requesting they stop sending the magazine seems to do the trick on the hard to stop magazines.

Unsubscribe from at least one magazine today

SUMMARY

Tools:

- Your computer
- Maybe your phone
- A timer

Time Estimate: 30 minutes or less to unsubscribe from one magazine.

Add Notes Here ↘

Commit to stopping the flow of emails

You created a home for your mail and registered to stop much of the unsolicited junk mail and pre-screened credit offers from getting into your mailbox (Steps #3 and #4). Excellent!

You gathered, sorted, and unsubscribed your magazines and catalogs (Steps #5 through #8). You established guidelines and set read-by dates so that your pile of reading material is both realistic and current. Congratulations!

The vision must be followed by the venture. It is not enough to stare up the steps, we must step up the stairs.

Vance Havner

Today's step is about slowing the flow of emails into your inbox. Emails are not paper, I know, but I see a lot of emails printed out, which adds to the paper piles. Besides, if you're busy reading your emails you may not have time to read your magazines, books, and other printed material, so those items end up adding to the paper piles.

We are information-seeking creatures. It makes sense to keep learning and gathering information. However, information is only useful if you can access it, use it, and share it. If you haven't had time to read it or act on it, the information coming in is not useful. It's not achieving its purpose or improving your life.

Here are the top seven strategies for gaining control of your email inbox:

1. Delete your email account and create a new one. Yes, this is drastic, but think of it as a do-over. You now have a better idea of what you read and what you're interested in so you won't have last year's interests mixing with today's priorities. When I had to kill the business email account that I had had for ten years and start over, I was initially frustrated and angry. The following week, when I had only prospect and client emails to read, was one of the most relaxing, non-vacation weeks I've had.

2. Create a "junk" email account that you use only for unimportant sign-ups. The ones where, in order to get a VIP card for the store, you have to give them an email; then the store sends a weekly promotional email. This "junk" email account allows you to access the emails when you want, without overwhelming your inbox when you're looking for the personal or business message you need.

3. Create filters or rules that send emails from specific senders or subjects to a folder automatically. Most email servers have this option. For example: Outlook® uses the term 'rule' and the term 'filter' is used by Gmail™.

4. Unsubscribe email by email. Every marketing email or email list you subscribed to should have a link that allows you to unsubscribe. Pick an email and click the link. I've found that most of the unsubscribes work great and only one or two don't seem to actually unsubscribe me. If an email continues to come after unsubscribe — block it or create a filter or rule to have it sent directly to your trash.

5. Use the Email Preference Service (eMPS) to remove your email from national lists. eMPS is a consumer service sponsored by the Data & Marketing Association (DMA). Go to DMAchoice.org and scroll to the bottom. Below the main header image is a section entitled "More Than Just Mail" and you will find the link for *Email Opt Out Service*. Or you can go directly to www.ims-dm.com/cgi/optoutemps.php.

6. Check out Unroll.me to see if this service will work for you. Unroll.me is a free service that will identify your subscription emails, allow you to unsubscribe to ones you no longer want and create a daily digest email, called the Rollup. Pros: you get to stay subscribed to emails you want, look through the daily digest when you want, and keep your inbox clear. Cons: You provide your email username and password to Unroll.me to allow them access to identify subscription email and roll it up into the daily digest. This is one more access point for

malware or computer virus. Other issues voiced on discussion sites include: a one-time requirement to share on social media; and all the emails that were rolled up and taken out of the inbox return to the inbox when you close your Unroll.me account. I don't use Unroll.me but I've heard from fellow organizers that they love it. I want to at least introduce you to this tool so that you can make the decision for yourself.

7. Do nothing. Doing nothing to stop the flow of emails is always an option you can choose. Once you decide to allow the emails to keep coming, you do have some options to maintain control of your inbox.

    - Ignore it. Who says you can't have 10,549 emails in your inbox and still be relaxed and at peace? Decide to ignore the number and change your expectations.

    - Delete it. You can delete email by email. Every once in a while, you can sort your emails by date and delete anything older than 3-months, 12-months, 2-years, or whatever dead-by date you set. A dead-by date is the length of time you're comfortable with setting, believing you won't need the email again. It's probably longer than it needs to be, but start somewhere and evaluate as you go.

    - Move it and then delete it. You could create a folder and move old emails (read and unread) into it. Set a dead-by date and then delete the folder. I always suggest naming the folder your dead-by date so you know when to delete it.

Pick one or more of these strategies and begin to stop the flow of email. The idea is not to stop all paper and information from coming in but to reduce the flow to a manageable stream. Somewhat like going from a fire hose to a garden hose to eventually a soaker hose.

Which strategy will you use to stop the flow?
_____

You will also free up your time to do the fun things you've been waiting to do. Your home, your in-box, your mail and your magazines, and even your to-do list will be clear of unimportant and unwanted paperwork. You'll be able to focus on the priorities. Think of this as inviting only your friends to stay, or allowing the A-listed information to cross the threshold while keeping the B-listed items out at the curb.

SUMMARY

Tools:

- Your computer
- A timer

Time Estimate: You probably already know that this step can take as much time as you allow it. Decide whether you're going to work on this step for 15 minutes, 30 minutes, or more. Set your timer and do it in 15-minute blocks of time. The timer will remind you to STOP reading and keep deleting, moving, or sorting.

Choose a strategy to stop the flow of emails

Implement the chosen strategy

Add Notes Here ⬂

Create a mobile mail processing kit

You have options here. Do you want an established space to process your mail (and bills) or do you want to be mobile? Of course, you can have both, but creating a mobile **Mail Processing Kit** gives you flexibility. Choose a basket or box that's easy to handle. Add envelopes, stamps, pens, checkbook, letter opener if you want, staple remover, note cards if you need, sticky notes, and maybe a pair of scissors. You can add a mini stapler to your box for just a few bucks. THIS will be your MAIN processing toolkit.

Stay committed to your decisions, but stay flexible in your approach.

Tom Robbins

I find that my IRIS project case is a perfect size. It encloses the items and I can shelve it on its side where it takes up less room. It also provides a flat surface if I need one to write on. I've labeled it, but since it's clear I can easily see what's in it. The IRIS project cases are usually available from your local office supply store or hobby shop, but check out any store that carries plastic containers. Amazon.com is always an option.

Don't rush out and buy the project case. For now, find a box with a lid that can hold your paper processing supplies and can easily be moved without dumping it. As you use it, you'll learn what else you need and if mobile works for you. Once you've determined what you need, put it on your shopping list in Appendix B.

Choose a temporary container for your **Mail Processing Kit**

Add:

- Checkbook
- Envelopes
- Stamps
- Address labels
- Pens
- Letter opener
- Stapler
- Staple remover
- Stationery
- Sticky notes
- Marker
- Scissors
- And more (or less)

Recommended product:

- IRIS Project Case

SUMMARY

Tools:

- Basket, box, or container
- A timer

What you put in your **Mail Processing Kit** is up to you. These items are only options.

- Address labels
- Checkbook
- Envelopes
- Letter opener
- Pens
- Scissors
- Stamps
- Staple remover
- Stapler
- Stationery
- Sticky notes

Time Estimate: Building your mail processing kit may take 30 minutes to find a temporary container and collect all the items you'll need. Before you purchase a new container, create a temporary mail processing kit and test it out.

Add Notes Here ↘

Choose an initial paper storage unit

Do you already have file drawers that you want to use as your primary paper storage? Is there plenty of space to add new files or are they overflowing with paper? Are you worried that clearing them out would be a project all by itself? No worries.

We'll get to clearing those drawers and boxes of paper in Step #30, but for now, you'll need an initial or temporary paper storage unit. It will get you started while you are establishing new guidelines (Step #14) and behaviors. Once you cull your papers, you may decide to keep this temporary unit and make it permanent.

One file box or file drawer should be sufficient for routine mail processing. Here's what you need to look for if you choose a file box: a good seal, sturdy walls and handles, and easy, one-handed opening (you're going to have paper in the other hand).

When it comes to storing your papers, spend the money on the tools that will last and withstand constant use. Nothing is more irritating than a drawer that won't open easily, a lid that keeps falling off, or a container that won't close.

I recommend the IRIS watertight mobile file box or watertight bankers box that hold hanging folders. I like the IRIS products. They're sturdy, they're clear, and I like the feel. They're also made in the USA. Appendix B has a list of products I recommend.

Nobody can go back and start a new beginning, but anyone can start today and make a new ending.

Maria Robinson

Choose your file box

Check out Appendix B for additional items to shop for

Recommended product:

- IRIS Watertight Mobile File Box

SUMMARY

Tools:

- Sturdy file box
- A timer

Time Estimate: You might have an empty file box available, but if not you will have to purchase this. Check out the shopping list in Appendix B to see what other items you may need. These steps are meant to be done one at a time, but if you need tools and resources, it makes more sense to take one trip to the store rather than several. Now may be the time to look for the various home containers if you need to change them out.

Add Notes Here ↘

Build in maintenance

Simplify your filing system and build in the file maintenance. You may have gone paperless on some bills and statements. For those paper bills that you choose to keep coming, you'll need a filing system that makes maintenance easy. After all, lack of maintenance is one of the main reasons your paper has been piling up. You will establish your **Keep or Toss** guidelines in Step #14, but today you're constructing your initial file categories and systems, which builds in the maintenance.

The road to success is always under construction.

Lily Tomlin

Label twelve hanging folders with the months of the year (**January - December**).

Instead of filing by vendor or payee, file your statements and paid bills by month. Of course, you may not need to keep the statement at all, but if you want to hold onto it, you've built in the maintenance. Each month you can pull out last year's paper and shred it before filing this year's. For example, it's March; pull out last year's March bills and statements from the **March** folder, shred, and then file this year's March statements as you pay or review them. If you choose, you can quickly flip through the folder's contents and pull out anything that should have been dropped in a different folder, such as taxes.

As you pay your bills, review your statements, or file your receipts, you can open up the current month's folder and drop the paperwork inside. No more searching for the labeled folder for each utility or bill only to find that it's too full.

What happens if you need to find the electric bill from last July? You may be worried you might have to go digging through the July folder. You're right; you would have to sort through the other July bills to find it, but that should only take a minute or two at the most because you filed it rather than just putting it in that pile to file later. You know exactly where the file is!

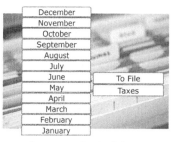

Step #12: Folders Monthly + Taxes + To File

Two more hanging folders to create at this time.

Label one folder **Taxes**. As you bring in paper (mail or receipts) that are tax related, drop it in this folder. Anything tax related goes here (statements, receipts, or documents). You'll build your tax archive folders in Step #21.

Label the second folder **To File**. As you process your mail and incoming paper, drop in any paper you want to keep for reference that doesn't belong in the **Monthly** folders or the **Taxes** folder. Before you do, put a sticky note on the paper and jot down a word or two to describe it. The note will help in identifying the category when we get to this **To File** folder in Step #24.

I've left the decision of printing or writing the labels up to you. Some prefer the clean, consistent type of a labeler while others enjoy connecting with the categories by writing the label. I don't recommend using your computer and printer to print out the labels. Unless you do labels on your printer routinely, it could take you hours to get your files labeled. Make sure the print is as large as you can make it and easily readable. Consider using the month abbreviations (JAN, FEB, MAR, etc.) to make the print on the label as big as possible. The bigger the print, the easier it is to identify the correct folder.

Place the tab on the side of the folder nearest you so that you can grab the label and pull the folder towards you. This makes opening the folder easier and your filing quicker.

Placing the folder tab on the near side of the folder allows you to pull the folder open.

If you choose colored folders, buy an extra bag or two of the clear, colorless label tabs. The colored tabs make it harder to see written or printed labels. Keep it simple.

In this step, I've only mentioned hanging folders. I don't recommend using file folders inside hanging folders. Using both the hanging and the file folders would require twice as much labeling and work.

SUMMARY

Tools:

- At least 14 sturdy hanging folders
- Clear, non-colored folder labels or tabs
- Pen
- Marker or a labeler
- A timer

Time Estimate: 30 minutes if you have the folders already.

Add Notes Here ⬂

Create **Monthly** folders

Create **Taxes** and **To File** folders

- At least 14 hanging folders

Note: I don't recommend using the store brand hanging folders. My experience with "store" brand paper & office products has been

13 To Shred or Not to Shred

I can't change the direction of the wind, but I can adjust my sails to always reach my destination.

Jimmy Dean

Do you have to shred everything? Since the goal of shredding is to prevent others from easily stealing your personal and financial information from your mail, documents, and other paperwork, part of the answer is straightforward. If it has your social security number, account number, or other private financial information that you wouldn't give even to a close friend — shred it. If you routinely register for giveaways, catalogs, or membership cards and don't think twice before giving them your address, phone, or email — you might decide not to bother with shredding that information. The information is already out there.

The other part of the answer is based on your comfort level and how much time you have to dedicate to the process. Today's step will help you establish your paper destruction guidelines so that you can take action and stop the piles from growing. Even the delayed decisions come with a risk that your information might be stolen from the pile.

Research Shredding Options

Do you buy a shredder or can you delegate that to a certified shredding company? If you purchase a shredder, choose cross-cut or micro-cut. I recommend getting at least a medium duty or heavy duty model. Look for the number of sheets it can handle at one time as well as the recommended continuous run time. Most light duty models can handle only a few sheets at a time and shouldn't be used longer than 10 minutes at a time. That's fine if you're caught up on your shredding and only need to do a handful at a time.

Of the brands that are usually available at your local office supply store, I only recommend Fellowes shredders. Don't buy the store brand. You get what you pay for and this is one item that you want to make your life easier, do the job well, and keep shredding for years to come.

Another option is a local shredding company or office store that offers shredding services. Check out the details and ask questions. You may have a local company that is certified and provides job training for special populations. Choose a company you trust. Look for a National Association for Information Destruction (NAID) AAA Certified Member at directory.naidonline.org.

> Look for a shredding company certified by the National Association for Information Destruction (NAID) at naidonline.org

If you are sorting through years of delayed paper decisions, it may make more sense (for your pocketbook and your time) to use a shredding company until you are firmly in the maintenance mode of your paperwork system.

Establish Your Shredding Guidelines

For some individuals, anything with their address on it needs to be destroyed (shredded, or the address removed or blacked out). For others, only financial and medical information needs to be destroyed. I do recommend shredding all credit card receipts that have the last four digits of your account number. The last four digits are often used to verify your account.

Estimate the time it will take and the protection it will give, then set your guidelines. Here are some questions to ask to determine if it's worth your time to destroy mail with your address:

- How much time am I willing to dedicate to destroying that information on every label, envelope, and paper?

- Do I commonly give out my address, phone number, or email? My address is already out there.

- Do I receive a lot of junk mail and catalogs? My address is already out there.

- Is my address visible on the Internet?

    You can find out by completing a search for your name. Check out some of the sites to see what information they have on you. If a site requests that you enter the name to search, don't. This is one way they get their information — **you** entering the search term on their website. Instead, go back to Google.com and enter your name and the website name in the search window.

Though removing your personal information from the internet is not a goal of this book, here are some resources to look at if you want to attempt it. I use the word 'attempt' intentionally. It's difficult, time consuming, and frustrating.

Enter the search term "if I find my address on the web how can I get it removed" or something similar in your browser search window. Read a couple of the articles to identify one step you can take. It's a process that will take time and patience.

Two articles I use as references are

- www.cnet.com/how-to/remove-delete-yourself-from-the-internet

- www.zdnet.com/article/how-to-remove-yourself-from-people-search-websites

Shred It

Once you have your shredding guidelines established and you've determined whether you're going to use a shredding machine or a shredding company, it is time to establish **when** you will shred.

During: You'll need to place your shredder near where you sort or process your paper. Shredding during paper processing is the best option as there is less likelihood of paper piling up in a to-shred box.

After: You will need to add an additional 10-15 minutes to your sorting or processing time to ensure that this step gets done and not left to later.

If you're doing the shredding, when will you do it?

Later: Saving the to-shred paper for later is not recommended unless you've decided to use a shredding company. If you save the pile for *later* shredding on your machine, *later* often never comes. The pile continues to grow, and it could become mixed with non-shredding items.

SUMMARY

Tools:

- A shredder if you've decided to do the shredding
- A box or container if you're using a shredding company
- A timer

Time Estimate: It may take an hour today to determine how, what, and when you'll shred.

Choose Shredder: look at online review such as on Amazon.com — limit it to 15 minutes.

Choose Shredding Company: Keep it to 30 minutes or less. Decide if the company will pick up your shredding (if that's an option) or if you'll drop it off.

Shredding: Limited based on your machine or distance to take shredding

Add Notes Here ⤵

If you purchase a shredder choose:

- Cross-cut or micro-cut
- Medium or heavy duty
- Compare number of sheets it can handle
- Compare continuous run time

Recommended brand: Fellowes

Use directory.naidonline.org to find a reputable shredding company.

Determine what you'll shred (shredding guidelines)

Keep or Toss?
Create guidelines

If you must play, decide on three things at the start: the rules of the game, the stakes, and the quitting time.

Chinese Proverb

Making a decision takes energy — a lot of brain energy. When you sort through your papers to decide whether to keep or toss, each paper becomes a decision. One box could potentially hold 3000 decisions — that's a lot of energy. It's no wonder you put off making the decisions, or if you do start sorting, you give up after a short time.

Two things can help you decrease the energy requirement and make the decisions easier:

The first is to have a set of questions to work through when facing a paper decision. Here's what I ask:

1. **Why do I need this?** Taxes, vital record, or legal requirement? Verify payment, purchase, or deposit? Memento or keepsake?

2. **How long do I need to keep it?**

3. **Can I find this information somewhere else?**

4. **How easy would it be to replace?**

5. **What was its purpose in my life? Is that purpose relevant today? Has it achieved its purpose?**

6. **If I keep it, how will I find it again?**

Download postcard-size copy of the **Paper Questions** at dhucks.com/resources31smallsteps_paper

If you'd like a postcard-size copy of these **Paper Questions**, go to www.dhucks.com/resources31smallsteps_paper to download your copy today or email simplify@dhucks.com.

The second tool that will help with decisions is a written (or printed) guideline for general paper categories. This is your **Keep or Toss Guide**. You will use it to establish the retention guidelines for your paper (and even electronic) documents.

You'll create these guidelines the first time as you decide how long you need and want to keep certain documents (paper question #2), as well as where they will be found (paper question #6). This will take energy and focus the first time, but after that, all you have to do is refer to your guide. Write your guidelines down, create a spreadsheet, or generate a list. Remember to note the purpose of the paper on your **Keep or Toss Guide**. I've created a pdf document that you could use to record your decisions. Go to www.dhucks.com/resources31smallsteps_paper to download your copy.

To help you find the answers that work for you, I've created a free step-by-step walkthrough on how to use the form, where to find the information that can help you make your decisions, and how to build your **Keep or Toss Guide**. Go to www.hyh.thinkific.com/courses/building-your-keep-or-toss-guide or just click on the course link next to the download link for the **Keep or Toss Guide** above.

Download pdf copy of the **Keep or Toss Guide** at dhucks.com/resources31 smallsteps_paper

Today's step was to establish the questions you need to ask when deciding whether to keep or toss papers and to develop the guidelines you'll follow when you're making a decision. As you sort and decide what to do with each piece of paper, review your questions and guidelines. Add categories and specific items as you need so that your guidelines are an active part of your paper processing and stay up-to-date. Place the guidelines in the front of your temporary filing box. The questions can go there also, or post them in a prominent spot near where you process your mail.

The goal of the **Keep or Toss Guide** is to lower the energy requirement of decision making. If you've decided that all utility bills are handled one way, then as they come in, you don't have to ask the questions, you can just jump into action.

Reminder: "Toss" is a general term that is used to describe the options for disposal in the trash, recycle, shredding, or giveaway.

Go to www.dhucks.com/resources31smallsteps_paper to download your free copies:

- **Paper Questions**
- **Keep or Toss Guide**

Or create your own questions and guide

Take free course on how to build your **Keep or Toss Guide** www.hyh.thinkific.com/courses/building-your-keep-or-toss-guide

SUMMARY

Tools:

- A pen and paper, or
- A computer and print out
- **Paper Questions**
- **Keep or Toss Guide**
- A timer

Time Estimate: 5 - 10 minutes to copy and print out the **Paper Questions**. Another 5 minutes to print out the **Keep or Toss Guide**. Take 30 minutes today to set some of your guidelines. Establishing more retention guidelines will happen over time as you make decisions on your paper.

The free course on building your **Keep or Toss Guide** will take approximately 45 minutes. You don't have to do it all at once.

Add Notes Here ⬋

Start at the end

As you began to take these small steps, you made an initial estimate of how much time you were willing to put into **maintaining** your paperwork. That block of maintenance time was also the minimum amount of time you committed to sorting, deciding and organizing your paper. How much time did you estimate? How many minutes or hours? Was that daily, weekly, or monthly?

How is your estimate working? Are you able to **maintain** the progress you've made? Yes, you still have a way to go (16 more steps as a matter of fact), but do you think that the minimum **maintenance** time requirement that you set at the beginning is reasonable and will be sufficient? Does that give you enough time to do the administrative work you need to do? Do you need to increase the minimum, or decrease it? Are you willing to spend that time? Can you stay focused for that long at one sitting or will you need to break it up into smaller blocks of time more often?

This step is entitled "Start at the End" because I want you to think ahead to when you've worked through your piles and your boxes are gone. You will focus on **maintaining** the processing of the paper that is coming in. How much time will your paper system take you to **maintain**? Are you willing to spend that time? Are you?

If you don't want to put in that time, you'll have to simplify. Though easy access to your papers and the information they contain is a goal, your ultimate goal is probably to enjoy more free time, reach for your dreams, and live your life on *purpose*. Your system needs to support that goal, not take away from it.

Start at the end to determine how much time you're willing to spend on paper; then build your system to support your commitment.

Start where you are. Use what you have. Do what you can.

Arthur Ashe

How much time did you commit to your paper management back at the start of this journey?

_____

How much time are you willing to commit to your paper management now?

_____

The terms **maintain**, **maintaining**, and **maintenance** are bolded because your time estimate is geared solely for the incoming mail and papers. When you still have a backlog of paper in piles, boxes, and drawers, you will need to put in extra time to work through it. But if you're not willing to do the minimum maintenance in the end, you'll never dig out from under your piles now. If the term "maintenance" slows you down, think of this as **practice** instead. You are practicing your organizing skills in each session.

SUMMARY

Tools:

- A peaceful spot to decide
- Pen and paper to jot down your time commitment
- A journal if you want to investigate conflicting thoughts
- A timer

Time Estimate: 15 minutes to evaluate whether your initial time commitment to **maintaining** paperwork is realistic and doable. Less than a minute to recommit to your new time block.

Add Notes Here ⬇

Recommit to your time block.

Schedule the next **maintenance** or **practice** session now.

Set aside a specific day

Now that you have established how much maintenance time you'll need, you'll want to set a specific day or days that you'll do your mail or paper processing. Will it be every week, twice a month, or once a month? When? The 15th and the 30th? Every Saturday? In the morning, after work, or in the evening? Once you've set your time and day(s), put it on your calendar, then keep that appointment. Do it.

If you find you often push back that appointment, evaluate and determine if you need to change your routine mail processing day to a more realistic time, or do you need help in keeping that commitment? Would you be willing to establish an accountability partnership with a friend, supportive group, or professional (organizer, coach, or therapist)? Often, we don't hold appointments and commitments to ourselves unless we've committed to someone else first.

If you're only willing to spend one hour twice a month for filing, bill paying, and maintenance, great. Start with that to see if it's realistic and doable.

It doesn't matter what you can do. What matters is what you will do.

Robert Anthony

When will you schedule your Mail Processing appointment(s)? Set a day and a time.

_____

- Determine the best day or days for mail processing.

- Schedule your next two Mail Processing dates.

- Commit to a friend or professional.

- Remain open to learning if that day works.

SUMMARY

Tools:

- Your calendar or planner to schedule the mail processing appointment
- A phone to ask a friend or hire a professional to help
- A timer

Time Estimate: 5 minutes to determine the best days and 2 minutes to schedule the next two paper dates in your planner/calendar. A reminder that this is still an experiment so you can change routine mail processing days until you find one that you can commit to.

Add Notes Here ↘

Test your paper maintenance system

Grab your **Mail Home** (Step #3), your **Mail Processing Kit** (Step #10), your retention guidelines from Step #14, and your file box (if it's mobile, Step #11). Today you're going to test your paper maintenance system by paying your bills, unsubscribing from another catalog you don't want, shredding incoming paper you won't keep, etc. Remember to add some fun (music, movement, light, even your favorite beverage, etc.) and make it more social if you can. The goal is to find what's missing, what doesn't work, and what needs to be tweaked.

When it is obvious that the goals cannot be reached, don't adjust the goals, adjust the action steps.
— Confucius

Set your timer for the time you said you were willing to do in one sitting (Step #15). Go! Process your paperwork. Stop the timer if you need to add something to your kit or box. Go. Process, pay, file, schedule, decide. When the time is done, determine realistically if your system needs to be simplified, whether you need more practice to get the time down, or whether you have to increase the time that you commit to keeping your paper organized. Do you need to tweak the paper dates you scheduled in Step #16?

Any magazines or catalogs in the **Mail Home**? Take the ones to read and drop them in the **Magazine Home** with a clear read-by date assigned on a sticky note or directly on the cover.

Grab your paper processing tools, **Mail Home**, **Magazine Home** and test your guidelines and systems.

SUMMARY

Tools:

- Your **Mail Home** (Step #3)
- Your **Magazine & Catalog Home(s)** (Step #5)
- Mobile processing center (Step #10)
- **Paper Questions** (Step #14)
- **Keep or Toss Guide** (Step #14)
- Magazine & Catalog retention guidelines (Step #5)
- Your initial paper storage unit. (Step #11)
- A timer

Time Estimate: _____ minutes (fill in your time block) plus an estimated 30 additional minutes to update and revise your tools.

Add Notes Here ↘

Go paperless — carefully

When you think of going paperless, think LESS paper, not paperFREE. For some, achieving 90% paper free is doable. But for most of us, that's not realistic. And for many, I don't recommend it. I suggest that when you go paperless, you go carefully and proceed one step at a time so that you can assess and evaluate how it's working for you.

It is better to take many small steps in the right direction than to make a great leap forward only to stumble backward

Chinese Proverb

There are two parts to going paperless. One part is making payments paperless (no checks and no sending payments via mail). The other part is receiving statements and documents electronically.

Paperless Payment

If you're comfortable with technology and paying online, then you're probably already doing this. If you're not comfortable, start with one bill to learn and gain your confidence. Instead of deciding that all bills will be paid automatically, look at your reasons and evaluate individually. Choosing automatic payments for your mortgage/rent and necessary utilities (power & gas) is probably the best choice to start with. These are important expenses that you don't want to forget. They are usually the same amount each month or close. Yes, electric and gas may fluctuate season to season, but you can estimate these expenses. Credit card payments will vary depending on your balance and purchases. Not all credit card companies allow you to set payment at the minimum payment option. Some companies will "pull" an automatic payment even if your balance is zero. Check before you opt-in to a paperless payment. The bottom line is to determine why you want (or don't want) to pay electronically and move forward a step (or a bill) at a time.

Paperless Statements

Though paper is one of the biggest challenges we face because it is continually entering our lives and our homes, I don't always recommend going paperless with statements. Many banks require you to accept eStatements unless you want to pay a monthly fee. Saving money is a great reason to go paperless.

However, when it comes to discretionary spending and credit cards, getting your monthly statement in the USPS mail may save you money. Think about whether you're more likely to review your monthly purchases if the statement comes in the mail than if it comes in your overloaded email inbox. Reviewing your monthly statement can identify recurring expenses, such as magazine subscriptions, that you no longer need or use. You can then take action to turn them off or get a better plan that fits your needs.

Reviewing your monthly statements will also help you identify fraudulent purchases in time to take action and challenge the purchase. If the statement alert goes to your inbox instead and you don't make an effort to go to the credit card website, log-in, download the PDF statement, and review it on your computer, months may go by before you're aware something is wrong and by then it may be too late.

Align your decision to go paperless with your financial goals.

If you agree to receive paperless statements and plan to use the email statements to remind you to pay, you may overlook them if your inbox fills up. You could miss a payment and have to pay the fees and maybe even risk an interest rate increase.

If you want to go paperless on payments, start by setting up just one today. Time it. Add that much time to the next paper date so that you can schedule another bill to go paperless.

SUMMARY

Tools:

- Computer

- At least one bill from your **Mail Home**

- A timer

Time Estimate: 20 minutes for each bill or account that you change to paperless. It may be less for some accounts as they often have a pop-up window as soon as you sign-in that asks if you want to go paperless. However, you'll also want to confirm your email, read the agreement contract (yes, read the whole thing), and enter any financial information you need to pay online.

> Grab a bill you want to make into an automatic payment.
>
> -or-
>
> Grab a statement you want to receive via email.
>
> Go paperless carefully and with intention.

Add Notes Here ⬇

Get your first 'Take Action' tool ready (your calendar)

A goal is a dream with a deadline.

Napoleon Hill

If you already have a calendar/planner that works for you, then your task today is to make sure that it is up-to-date with your routine schedule. Skip to the **Update your calendar or planner** section on the next page. If you don't have a calendar or your calendar isn't working, your goal is to develop your most valuable tool for taking action.

No Calendar or Your Calendar Isn't Working

If you don't have a calendar or planner now, or your latest choice isn't working for you, you'll need more than 30 minutes today.

You'll need to decide whether you would work best with a paper or an electronic calendar. Three questions to consider: 1) how do you need to view your time commitments; 2) how easy is it to set up and use; and 3) how will you take it with you if you need it.

Will you need the ability to zoom in and out? You may need a month view if you want to see the big picture. Or zoom out even more to see the next three months or a full year. You may need to zoom into a day or week view to add the space for maintenance.

Your calendar must be easy to set up and create events. If it takes hours and hours to learn how to set up your calendar, and then it takes more time to enter new meetings, it's not saving you time in the end. If it takes effort to maintain, you're likely to let it get out of control. You need it easy and simple.

Will you need to take it with you and have ALL your appointments up-to-date? Up until this point, your paper planner (yes, I said paper) may have been the better choice for you. Other than having to add recurring meetings by hand, paper is often the easiest and quickest. But paper is not always the easiest to take with you due to size, weight, or if you want to be hands-free. A calendar tool on your phone might be the easiest to take with you, but it's difficult to see the big picture and too easy to schedule two big commitments back to back. A calendar on your computer can offer a big picture, but will it sync easily with your phone? An electronic calendar may also be preferred if you need to share calendars with others (family, co-workers, assistants, bosses).

There is no perfect calendar, but there are calendars that might work better for you than others. Think about what's worked for you in the past, what your needs are now, and then choose to start with a calendar that is good enough. Remember there is no "perfect calendar." Tweak as you go and make it better. Check out the calendars I've listed in Appendix B — Shopping List.

Update Your Calendar or Planner

Fill in all the appointments and tasks that you routinely do on a certain day or at a particular time. The calendar is for time-bound projects and actions. Tasks that need to be done, but not at a specific time, will go on your to-do or task list in Step #20. Making sure that your routine tasks and appointments are on your calendar will help keep you from overbooking your day and allow you to see what your day is like before you commit to *one more thing*. You may choose to rearrange your appointments to add in something you want or need to do, but make sure that *you* remain a priority. Commit to keeping your exercise, health, and self-care appointments.

Add Time

Build in travel time to and from appointments and meetings. Adding adequate travel time from one appointment to the next will ensure that you arrive on time and calm, rather than late and flustered.

Add travel time into your schedule.

Give yourself time to transition from one activity to the next. It's important for you to be fully present in each activity. For example, if you're working out at the gym, you may need time to cool down, shower, and dress before you move on to the next activity. Or if you're working on a project and have a meeting in an hour, you will need to add in the travel time. You will also need to give yourself time to make a note of where you are in the project, jot down what your next step will be, clear the space if you've spread out, and grab what you need for the next meeting. Leaving no transition time to clear up and prep for the next task has contributed to your paper piles over time.

Another contributor to your paper piles has been going from meeting to meeting to meeting without adding in administrative time to send that email, file your notes or follow-up on an action item. Add in time for routine administration of tasks after each meeting. Start with 20 minutes. Fifteen minutes for admin and five minutes for you to breath, relax and start on the next task. Add more time as needed. I admit, adding in transition time won't be an easy habit to build, but it is necessary.

Add 15 minutes to each meeting for follow-up activities.

Use Color

Color coding your appointments, meetings, and time-bound tasks can make your calendar more fun and exciting, which in turn will encourage you to use it more. Assigning a color to different categories can also help you identify certain appointments. You might use your favorite color for all self-care appointments (exercise, massage, doctors), green (money) or red (attention) for clients and customers. One of my clients used her favorite color for tasks and appointments she dreaded most. The color attracted her to take action. It also helped her change her perception of the task. With a paper calendar, you can use colored pens and pencils. Most electronic calendars allow you to categorize an appointment and assign colors to each category.

Though you may be eager to start working on your pile of action items today, don't. Yes, implement these ideas for tasks that come in from now on, but wait to work on the past items. You will be sorting your paper in Step #22 and taking action in Step #23. Today, celebrate your calendar. Practice using your calendar for the next two days. Add time-bound items as you go through your day. Schedule the commitments that have a specific date and time and are ones you want to do. Please remember to add in commitments to your health and happiness. Take time to relax, get a massage, enjoy a walk, or be with friends. Watch for what works and what doesn't. Make small changes as you need, but keep going.

Reminder: Place a reminder in your calendar to opt-out again in five years at DMAchoice.org and CatalogChoice.org.

SUMMARY

Tools:

- Calendar or planner
- Colored pens, pencils and even colored sticky notes if you're using a paper planner
- Computer, phone, or tablet if you're going electronic

Time Estimate: 30 minutes to get your calendar updated or an hour or more if you're starting from scratch.

Add Notes Here ↘

Decide paper or electronic.

Choose a calendar if you're not using one currently.

Update your calendar with routine appointments.

Add in travel time, transition time and follow-up or administration times.

Get your second 'Take Action' tool ready (your to-do list)

Things which matter most must never be at the mercy of those that matter the least.

Johann Wolfgang von Goethe

Your to-do list is a **Take Action** tool. It should not be the controlling force in your life, though it can help you achieve your dreams, decrease your stress, and free up your time. Your list is NOT a judge of what you must do tomorrow, of how well you did yesterday, or of what you should do now. It is a repository, a collection of random actions that may or may not be in order of priority. You need to look at your list and choose what's next. You are the one who determines the priority of the next task.

Must or Could

Stop thinking of a to-do list as a must-do list. Your to-do list is a tool to help you. It does not control your life, or at least it shouldn't. Your to-do list is a brain dump of activities and reminders and actions that you've thought about taking. It's a could-do list. It's a maybe-do-when-you-have-time list. It's a written list of tasks to choose from. Your to-do list will always have items on it. The goal is not to cross off (or check off) *all* the items. The goal is to take action on the most important ones, the priority items. Your to-do list allows you to see what's on your plate today or this week and make a conscious decision to do what's most important (hopefully) or do what's easiest (sometimes you need to enjoy an easy win). I'll be referring to your to-do list as a task list going forward.

Best Format

The best format for your task list is...whatever works for you. I recommend starting with paper. If you're already using electronic apps to track your tasks, then keep going. But if you don't have a task list, start with paper. A steno notebook, a brightly colored index card(s), or a sticky note on the bathroom mirror are just a few examples. Here are five situations to consider when establishing your task lists:

1) Do you get a feeling of accomplishment by crossing or checking off an item on your list? Paper usually is better for that. That sense of holding a pen or marker in your hand and making your mark fires many more neurons than does hitting a button on your phone.

   > Yes, it is okay to complete your task and then add it to your task list to cross it off.

2) Do you get overwhelmed by seeing too many tasks on your task list? Electronic lists might add to that feeling of overwhelm, so paper is a better choice. Keeping your day's task list on an index card and limiting it to 3 - 5 items can help. Writing one task per index card and sorting through the pack each week to find your priorities will include both visual cues (the written task) and movement (touching each task card as you sort) which can increase your willingness to decide and act.

3) Are you tired of re-writing your task lists? Electronic lists are best. You'll enter an item once and, depending on the app or software you use, it will keep moving to the current day until you mark it complete. You'll usually be able to look at your master task list and exclude completed tasks and projects or celebrate by seeing all that you've done.

4) Do you want to quickly search for keywords in a long list of tasks? Electronic is the way to go.

5) Would multiple lists be more helpful? Possibly. Or at least two lists: a master list for projects, goals, and tasks, and a task list for today. You might want a list for this week so that you keep the bigger picture in mind. A someday-maybe list can keep track of your possibility and dream ideas. Specific project lists can help you break down bigger tasks into manageable actions. And a list of actions to take when you're in the neighborhood might be created for different locales. Paper or electronic preference will depend on the type of list you create. However many lists you use, keep it simple enough to maintain.

Recommendations for Electronic Lists:

There are many options out there, here are four that I recommend are OneNote, Evernote, Trello, and KanbanFlow. Your calendar (paper or electronic) probably has a task option you can try out. Even your email might have a task tool associated with it.

Each task/to-do list app has its pros and cons. The next person you see using a productivity app, ask them what they're using. Check it out. Try it out. But don't spend a lot of time setting it up. And make sure the amount of time you'll spend maintaining your electronic list is worth it. The goal is not to organize your tasks but to get them done and off your list. Consider using the simplest option that helps you accomplish your tasks.

> Your list is NOT a judge of what you must do tomorrow, of how well you did yesterday, or of what you should do now.

Practice using your task list to empty your head of reminders and setting your priorities. Use your lists to increase focus on what you need and what you want to work on now.

How to Write It

Make sure you've included three things in your task item. What, when, and why.

What do you need to do? Start with a verb and put down your next step for the task.

When do you need to do it by? Of course, your calendar may be the best place for something that has a specific date, but your tasks usually have a "do-by date" that is important.

Why should you do it? If a task isn't supporting a goal or a priority or, most importantly, something you enjoy doing, why do it? The 'why' will help you identify the priority of the task.

SUMMARY

Tools: Choose your **Task List** tool(s)

- Sticky notes
- Index cards
- Steno pad
- Computer
- Phone
- Tablet
- Other tool

Time Estimate: 30 minutes to get your task list updated or started. Seriously, if you aren't able to start a list in under 30 minutes, it's too complicated for now. Go simpler.

> Decide the PRIMARY form for your **Task List**: electronic or paper.
>
> Try out a few and choose the easiest one to use and setup.
>
> Rename it – could-do list, task list, maybe list.
>
> Use your **Task List** repeatedly.

Add Notes Here ⬇

Get your filing tools together

Do not wait; the time will never be "just right." Start where you stand, and work with whatever tools you may have at your command, and better tools will be found as you go along.

Napoleon Hill

Your **Keep or Toss Guide** and your **Paper Questions** from Step #14 should already be in your paper storage unit. You've used the **Monthly** folders, current **Tax** folder and **To File** folders that you created in Step #12 for your mail and incoming paper. Today, you will create a paper storage unit for your reference or archives.

If you have file drawers that you want to use, but they're filled and unusable until you can sort through them, your second paper storage unit will be a temporary filing system. If you have no file drawers you want to use someday, then this unit will be the start of your permanent system.

Will you need a second file box in addition to your initial paper storage unit? If your initial paper storage unit is a small file box with a single handle and you have lots of paper that you think you want to keep, then yes, you will need a second, larger file storage box. However, if you started with the larger container or you have plans to keep only a little paper, then your smaller storage box may work just fine.

The goal of today's step is to create and label additional folders with the categories you need. Step #24 will be for the actual filing. You've had at least nine days (counting nine steps from when you created the basic categories - monthly, current taxes, and to file) to determine which papers coming in are ones you want to keep. Make your files as basic and as simple as you can so that maintenance and paper processing is easy and quick. If a folder is bulging from too much paper, consider one of the larger flat bottomed files with sides or break it up into more categories.

Here are a few general category suggestions:

Auto/Car   Insurance
Education/Work   Medical   Vital Records
Housing   Owner's Manuals*

Step #21: Folders Suggested Categories

* see Appendix D — Special Categories for going paperLESS

Add other folders based on the categories you've identified for the incoming papers. Some documents are better stored in a safety deposit box or fire-proof box instead of a common file box. Add other broad categories as needed. The intent is to keep the category broad enough to keep your filing simple, but narrow enough to find an item within a few minutes of searching through the folder.

Tax Archives (this may require a separate box)

You may intend to hold onto your tax returns and documentation for seven years, but it often turns into many more years than that because you never find the time to go through and clear away the out-of-date files. When you do make the time you usually find a drawer crammed full of paper and overstuffed folders. Usually, you've labeled the folder with "Tax yyyy" so a whole new label has to be made.

First, ask your tax accountant or read the IRS document, *How long should I keep records?* at www.irs.gov/businesses/small-businesses-self-employed/how-long-should-i-keep-records, to determine how long you need to keep your tax records. Then establish your keep guideline (add it to your **Keep or Toss Guide**).

How long will you keep your tax records?
_____

Though the IRS may only require that you keep records for three to seven years, I often recommend to clients a system that has built in the maintenance.

If you are going to keep the paper copies, set up ten flat-bottomed hanging folders. The color choice depends on your preference for cost and visual interest. Label the ten folders 0, 1, 2, ... through 9. Your 2016 taxes and documents will go in the hanging folder labeled "6". Your 2010 taxes go in "0" and so on. When 2024 taxes are done, you can then remove and shred the 2014 paperwork and plop in your 2024 papers, if you're still choosing to do paper returns that is. The maintenance is automatically built into your filing system, and you only have to get rid of one file at a time. Yes, you've kept your tax paperwork for longer than needed (assuming you don't need to keep it forever) but you've simplified your maintenance. No more relabeling, no more hours of shredding, and no more overflowing file drawers

Step #21: Folders Tax Archives, 0-9

Going PaperLESS

If you want to keep most of your references and archives electronically, you will want to take some time to plan how you're going to do it. Here are some basics:

Make sure your scanner can create OCR PDFs (that's Optical Character Recognition) and turn on the option. OCR allows the content of the PDF to be searched so that even if you don't remember what you named it, you can search for keywords in the document.

Set up a consistent naming format, such as *category company yyyy mm dd*. Examples: bank statement XYZcompany YYYY-MM-DD; home owners insurance policy ABCcompany YYYY-MM-DD.

Add as many keywords as you can think of to the file name. Twenty-four characters is no longer the limit on your filenames. The more keywords you add to the name, the quicker your computer search will be.

Set up your electronic files similar to your paper files. Don't create complicated subfolders within subfolders. Only enough to make sense to you. Remember you can search by a few keywords and let the computer do the heavy searching.

Another option is to set up your electronic files nothing like your paper files. You could keep all your files in one or at the most a handful of files and use the computer search function to find the file you're looking for. For many people, the suggestion to dump all your files into one folder is stressful, but consider it as a way of saving time by not clicking on one folder, then the next and the next; clicking away as you work your way through multiple layers on your computer.

You can scan and organize your documents in Step #24, **File It**. For now, you're building your electronic naming and filing system.

How will you name your electronic files?

_____

Step #21 to Organize Your Paper | 69

SUMMARY

Tools:

- Initial paper storage unit
- **Keep or Toss Guide**
- **Paper Questions**
- Pen/pencil
- Hanging folders, exact number determined by your categories
- 10 extra capacity or box-bottomed hanging folders
- Clear folder tabs/labels
- Labeler, if you want
- Possible second paper storage unit
- Copier/scanner, if you're going paperless

Time Estimate: 45 minutes to get your file archives started. If you want to create your paperless structure as well, add another 30 minutes.

Grab your

- Initial paper storage unit
- **Keep or Toss Guide**
- **Paper Questions**
- Pen
- Additional hanging folders
- 10 extra capacity or box-bottomed hanging folders
- Labels & labeler
- Second file box (maybe)
- Scanner if going paperless

Decide which broad categories you need.

Add Notes Here ⬇

Ready — Set — SORT

Habit is habit and not to be flung out of the window by any man, but coaxed down the stairs a step at a time.

Mark Twain

You've begun processing the incoming paper and mail; now to start sorting through the older piles of papers. Decide whether you'll sort these piles from the past for 15 minutes or an hour today. Or maybe some time in between. Add an extra 15 minutes at the end to clear the area and ensure that it's ready to use tomorrow.

You will sort into four main categories. Focus on sorting as quickly as you can. The goal for your time is to sort; not to read, not to take action, not to get lost in memories. SORT.

Sort into these four categories

Here's what goes in the four categories and their subcategories.

Let Go

This is a broad category of items that will be leaving your home in one of four ways:

- **Shred** — You'll add the paper that you don't want but has personal or financial information you want to keep private. Refer to your shredding guidelines from Step #13. Consider the term "shredding" to cover any alternatives you use to remove information in another way (i.e. blacking out the information).

- **Recycle** — Any paper that you don't need and don't need to shred can go here or in the trash, based on your local recycling options and choices.

- **Trash** — Add the paper you don't need, that doesn't need to be shredded, and that you won't or can't recycle.

- **Giveaway** — This category is for any items you come across that you don't want but someone does. Keep in mind, I just stated someone else *wants*. Don't clutter up their lives either. Before you put the paper or item in the **Giveaway** box, add a label so that you'll remember who gets it. Small sticky notes are perfect for this.

Take Action

- **Now** (today) — These are tasks that need immediate action because they've been sitting in the piles so long. Do not take action during your sorting time. If something needs to be done today, place a sticky note on it and write down the next step to take. Take action on this pile after your sorting time is completed and you've cleaned up.

- **Not Now** (later) — These are tasks that may need to be done but they don't need to be done today. Remember, do not take action on anything while you're sorting. You will jot down the next action to take and when you need to take it on a sticky note. Put the sticky note on the piece of paper. You'll be dealing with this **Not Now** pile tomorrow in Step #23.

> Focus on sorting as quickly as you can. No filing, no taking action, and definitely no reading. The timer is there to remind you to get back to sorting.

File It

This category is for those items that you want to access at a later date. Refer to your paper retention guidelines from step #14. By now you have a better idea of what you want to keep and what you don't need. We will address filing this stack of papers in Step #24. For now, you're simply sorting the paper into this category. Place a sticky note and write the file name on it to save time later when you file.

Though I'd prefer you wait to file until later, you might feel the need to file those items that you already have a labeled file or home for. If that's the case, go ahead, but do it *after* your sorting session. The filing can be part of your clean-up time. I urge you to limit your filing to *after* the sorting is done because, at this point, you might be easily distracted by a neighboring file and get off track.

To Be Revisited (TBR)

This category is also known as the "I'm not sure," "I don't know yet," "to ripen," or "haven't a clue" pile. Don't worry if it's the biggest pile. This category will naturally decrease over time as you develop your paper guidelines and build your decision muscle. Drop anything that doesn't fit in the first three categories into the **TBR** box.

Now that you know the categories, set up the sorting stations. Bring out a trash can, recycle container, your shredding box, and a container to hold the giveaways. You'll need a box for the **TBR** category as that's likely to be your largest pile and may take more time to deal with. Label it **TBR** or **To Be Revisited** and put today's date on it. The **File It** and the two **Take Action** categories, **Not Now** and **Now**, may only require a sheet of paper with the category written on it and placed on the floor or table to act as a target for the sorting. You could also use a box, basket, or tray for your drop zone.

Once you've set up your stations with the above categories and subcategories, grab an inch or two of papers and start sorting. Sort through a short stack (an inch or a handful) of papers rather than a full stack or box in front of you. This allows you to see that there is an end. You can easily get to the bottom of a handful of papers in 15 minutes; then celebrate.

Set your timer for 15 minutes (or your designated time block) and SORT. If you committed to working on your paper piles for longer than that, you'll work in multiple blocks of 15-minutes. If you only have seven minutes to sort, then set your timer for 7.

When your timer goes off, decide whether you're done sorting for the day, or if you want to go another 15 minutes. Save your last block of time for the cleanup.

Once you're done for the day and ready to clear your sorted categories to prepare your space for tomorrow, you will need to move the trash, recycle, and shred to their designated places. If you decided back in Step #13 that you will shred after each session, add that to your cleanup time.

Next, identify when you'll take the **giveaway** items to their soon-to-be new owners. Plan for sooner rather than later. Put it in your calendar or on your Task List (with a do-by date)

You sorted the **Take Action** pile into two piles: the things you need to take action on today (**Now**) and a "tomorrow & later" pile (**Not Now**). Step #23 will focus on the tomorrow & later action items, so put them off to the side for now. You can place these items in a box or container labeled **Take Action** or in the **Mail Home**. If you put them in the **Mail Home**, be sure to clip them together or somehow indicate they've been sorted and they're now items for action. For those items that you want to take action on today, do it after you've cleared your space for tomorrow.

Place the sorted **File It** papers either in a labeled box or container or label the stack and put it in your **Mail Home** for further processing in Step #24.

Put the **TBR** items in a labeled box or container. Step #25 covers processing your TBR box, but for now, put this aside also.

If you have a lot of boxes or stacks of papers that you want to sort through, it's going to take a while, but relax, you're committed to getting your papers in order. You committed to taking your space back. You want a more organized life so that you can spend your time doing what you love.

When is your next paper sorting session?

_____

Schedule your next paperwork sorting session. Sorting is going to be a rinse-repeat activity. You will need to schedule these sessions repeatedly until you get through your boxes and bags of delayed paper decisions. I will remind you later in the book to schedule paper sorting sessions, but consider making your paper sessions at least a weekly activity for now.

SUMMARY

Tools: Sorting bins/containers with labels as needed

- **Trash** can

- **Recycle** bin for paper

- **Shred** box — either to shred or to take to a shredding site

- Box for **Giveaway** — labeled

- Box for **Take Action** (**Not Now**) — labeled

- Tray or folder or target area for **Now** action items (after sorting session is completed)

- Box or folder or target area for **File It** — labeled

- Box for **TBR** — labeled

- Sticky notes

- Marker or pen (for writing the labels)

- Timer

Time Estimate: _____ minutes (write in your set administration time) + 15 minutes for clearing away the sorted piles.

Grab containers and label:

- Trash
- Recycle
- Shred
- Giveaway
- Action–**Now**
- Action–**Not Now**
- File
- TBR

SORT

Use sticky notes to provide reminders of who, where, what, when

---

Add Notes Here ↘

Take Action

Even if you're on the right track, you'll get run over if you just sit there.

Will Rogers

Add more hanging folders to your paper storage unit. Label one **Action Items**. This will be the home for any piece of paper you need to take action on once you've processed it and have decided that you still need to keep it. This is different from the **Take Action** box you filled in Step #22.

The second folder to create is a **TBR (To Be Revisited)** file. Label it. This folder is also for taking action, but the action is to decide later if you're going to take action or not. This may grow into a whole section by itself, but for now, it's going to be just one hanging folder.

Today you'll be moving the paper from your **Take Action** box (Step #22) into your action tools—your calendar (Step #19) and your task lists (Step #20) and possibly into one of the folders you just created today.

Step #23: Folders
Add two more

Get your **Take Action** box and grab the first piece of paper; confirm that you still want to take action. If you haven't already identified the next step to take, do so now.

Is there is a specific time and date associated with the action you want to take? If there is, enter that task or 'next step' into your calendar. An example would be a flyer for a local event that you want to attend. You'd make a calendar entry for the date and time. Add location and any other relevant information you'll need.

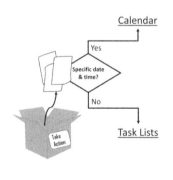

If there's no specific time, add it to your **Task List**. You could add it to either your **Now** task list (today's tasks) or your **Not Now** task list, aka master task list. A coupon from your local electric company to call to schedule their free home energy assessment would be added to your task list as a reminder.

Once you've added your **Take Action** papers to your calendar and your list(s), you may find that you don't have time to do everything you think you should or even want to do. You will prioritize, you may delegate, or you may even decide to say 'no' to the opportunity. You're building your decision muscle — excellent. Keep going.

Add the information you need from the piece of paper to the calendar or task list entry. Information like phone numbers, locations, individuals that you need to contact, web addresses, or other relevant details. If all the information is in your calendar or on your list, then you can let go of that piece of paper.

Action Items Folder

If you still need that piece of paper, you'll need to put it where you can find it again. If it already has an identified home, then place it there. If not, put it in the **Action Items** folder. This is the home for all papers that have been entered into your calendar or task lists and that you don't otherwise have a designated location for. When you need it, this is where you'll find it. Maybe that flyer for the local event you added to your calendar had more than just the date, time and location. You might want to refer to the detailed schedule of the day's events that are listed. You would then keep the paper and drop it in the **Action Items** folder.

> The **Action Items** folder is a temporary home for paper information related to an item that is on your calendar or task list.

Make a note on the calendar entry or the task list that the paper is in the **Action Items** folder. A simple 'AI' might be enough to remind you to look in the folder when you need it. Once you've accomplished the task or project, you can toss the paper.

You will need to go through the **Action Items** folder every once in a while to make sure that you've cleared away completed items. Add a recurring entry to your calendar every two or three months to cull this file. The last Friday of the month might be perfect to schedule some file maintenance time on your **Action Items**.

The next time you go through the **Action Items** folder, evaluate the process and your decision muscle. If you find that you have lots of completed items, this may mean that you didn't need the paper as you thought. If you find that you have lots of uncompleted items with deadlines that have passed, then determine what part of the calendar or your task list system isn't working. Or maybe you decided later that you didn't truly want to do it after all. Your decision muscle is growing, and the next sorting session will have more going into the **To Be Revisited** pile or even the **Let Go** pile. Either way, congratulations! You're making progress, and your decision muscle is growing stronger.

Here's a recap of the Take Action process:

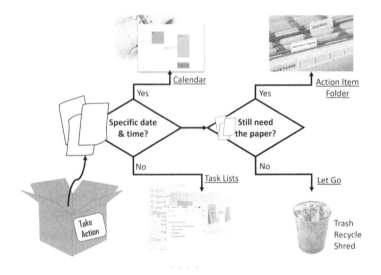

NOTE: You may or may not have heard of a tickler file. It's usually a set of files or pockets numbered 1 through 31 and may include an additional 12 labeled **January** through **December**. Some individuals would use a Tickler File to put those tasks and projects in instead of the one folder we've labeled **Action Items**. I recommend starting with the simpler, single folder. With a tickler file, you have to remember to look at each day and each month. With a single folder and your tasks either on your task list or your calendar, it won't take much time to go through to find the piece of paper you want, and it takes up less space in your file storage unit.

To Be Revisited (TBR)

When you sorted the first time you may have thought you wanted to take action on a particular piece of paper, but maybe the second time you look at it you're not so sure. If you're not yet certain you want to take action, drop the paper in the **TBR** folder. This is where the *someday, maybe* ideas go. Maybe you have an article on a new hobby you might want to take up *someday* — drop it in the **TBR** folder. Maybe you have instructions on how to create something for your business, but you're not sure you want to do it now — toss it in the **TBR** folder.

Place your *someday, maybe, when I have time,* opportunities and ideas in the **To Be Revisited (TBR)** file instead of creating a new file for each possibility. You will want to touch these papers again and again until you decide to toss it or do it. This is a place for the idea to ripen and not get lost in the piles. The possibilities now have a home.

You will also have to go through this file every couple of months. You'll touch each paper again and decide to let go, act on it, or put it back. Write the date on the paper each time you put it back. If you have not acted on it in 6 months, a year, or whatever deadline you set, then let it go because more ideas will come.

At this point, you've scheduled tasks on your calendar that have a specific time and date associated with the action. You've dealt with those tasks or projects that don't have a specific time by getting it out of your paper piles and onto your task list. You have also placed those pieces of paper that you aren't ready to act on and you're not letting go in a home of their own (**TBR**). Congrats!

You took this step today on old paper. As you process your mail and the paper you bring into your life going forward, you will Take Action for each paper as it enters your life. You no longer have to pile. Instead move the paper that requires action into your calendar, task list, or the To Be Revisited.

When's your next paper sorting session (Step #22)? You will need to repeat this Take Action step again and again as you continue to sort through your old piles of paper.

When is your next paper sorting session?
_____

Move the items from your **Take Action** box (or **Mail Home**) to your action tools

- Calendar for tasks with date or time demands
- **Now** task list for tasks that need to be done now but not at a defined time
- Master task list for **Not Now** actions
- **Actions Items** folder for paper that contains information that you can't enter in the calendar or the **Task List**
- **TBR** folder for paper awaiting a decision to

SUMMARY

Tools:

- Calendar
- To-do lists (**Now** and **Not Now** task lists)
- Sticky notes
- Pen/pencil
- Two new hanging folders and labels
- Your paper storage unit
- **Take Action** box
- **Mail Home**, if you clipped the **Take Action** papers together and dropped them in your **Mail Home**
- **Let Go** containers (trash, recycle, shred, giveaway)

Time Estimate: 30 minutes to get your **Take Action** papers scheduled in your calendar and task lists. Depending on how many take actions papers you have in the box, you may need to schedule more sessions. And more sorting sessions from Step #22 will lead to more items on your task lists and in your calendar. Prioritize and build your decision muscle.

Add Notes Here ⬇

File it

The goal of filing is not to store your papers but to access them when you need them. As you learned in Step #12, making your files easier to maintain is also key to finding what you need when you need it. Grab both your **To File** folder from Step #12 and your **File It** box from Step #22. Get your paper storage unit(s) which should include the folders you added in Step #21 and the **Keep or Toss** retention guide you developed in Step #14.

Today your focus is getting the 'to file' papers out of the **To File** folder and the **File It** box and into their home folders in your initial paper storage unit. Start with the **To File** folder as it contains the most current paperwork. Set your timer for 15 minutes or your designated working block of time and file.

If you come across a paper that doesn't have a folder yet, put it off to the side for now. Save 15 minutes at the end to create the additional folders you need. Focus on filing.

As you go through your **File It** box, reassess your need to keep each item. If it falls into a decision you already made in your **Keep or Toss Guide** that you created in Step #14, proceed to place it in its appropriate file or location. If you don't have guidance for the next piece of paper, then decide if you're keeping it and for how long. Add the decision to the guide. Today's step is about filing the paper and also expanding your **Keep or Toss Guide** as necessary.

For those items that you've decided you only need for a year, place them in your current month's folder. It's okay if you don't get every receipt and statement in the most appropriate month's folder. The goal is to get them in your **Monthly** files and out of the pile.

That which we persist in doing becomes easier for us to do; not that the nature of the thing itself is changed, but that our power to do is increased.

Ralph Waldo Emerson

Folders in your paper storage units

You probably have a limited amount of space for paper storage, which is why you created your **Keep or Toss Guide**. But it's also likely that you don't have enough room to keep all your files near where you process your incoming paper. You may need to store some of your paper resources and archives in a different room or a harder to access location. Before you place your files anywhere, think of how often you might need to access them.

A document that you access routinely, such as a phone directory or school schedule, should be placed in an easy to access location. Instead of filing it, maybe putting it in a notebook next to the phone or computer is the best place for it. You want to keep it where you use it and within arm's reach. For those documents and records that you rarely access, like tax records, you can place them in a different room or on a harder to reach shelf. See Appendix C for information on Organizing Zones.

Refer to Appendix C for more on establishing your organizing zones for paper.

You'll repeat this filing step as part of your regular mail processing routine and also when you have a **File It** pile built up from sorting through your old papers. This is not a one and done. Now that you are establishing your guidelines and building your decision muscle, this step will become easier and easier to take when the paper first comes into your life. There will be fewer delayed decisions causing a pileup. In addition, the time required to process the incoming paperwork will decrease as you maintain your organization system.

Once you're finished filing for the day, the last 15 minutes will be spent on making those additional folders you need. Grab those papers that you set aside because they didn't fit in any of the categories you had. Determine the new categories you'll need, keeping them as broad as possible so the folders hold multiples pieces of paper instead of making multiple folders that hold a single item each. Label the folders and file the papers.

PaperLESS

If you want to scan your paper documents and keep them electronically, today's step is the place to do it. Start scanning, and remember to use the naming format you established in Step #21.

Once you've begun to go paperLESS check out www.documentsnap.com. You'll find clear and easy to understand tips and instructions on going paperless. If you want more hands-on help in going paperless, contact a professional organizer for assistance. To find one in your city, search NAPO.net. You can also go to VirtualOrganizers.com to find an organizer who works virtually or off-site.

Grab your

- **To File** folder
- **File It** box
- Initial paper storage unit
- Second paper storage unit
- **Keep or Toss Guide**
- **Paper Questions**
- Timer
- Sticky notes
- Pen, marker or labeler
- Hanging folders
- Clear tabs or labels
- Scanner if going paperLESS

File

SUMMARY

Tools:

- Your initial paper storage unit with **Monthly** files and the **To File** folder (Step #12)

- Second paper storage unit with specific category folders (Step #21)

- **File It** box from Step #22

- **Keep or Toss Guide**

- **Paper Questions**

- Sticky notes

- Pen, marker or labeler

- More hanging folders and label tabs

- Scanner, if you decide to go paperLESS

- Timer

Time Estimate: 60 minutes to file the paper from the **To File** folder & **File It** box. Set your timer for 15-minute blocks to stay focused. Save the last 15 minutes to create needed folders and file remaining papers. Take 5 more minutes to schedule your next sorting session if you haven't already planned it.

Add Notes Here ⬊

25 TBR — To Be Revisited

One of the stacks you sorted into in Step #22 was the **To Be Revisited (TBR)**. This **TBR** stack is important. As you sort through your papers, I don't want you to get stuck or bogged down. I want you to keep moving forward; let go of the paper you don't want clogging up your space; give the paper you want to remain in your life a home; and more importantly, I want you to build your decision muscle on which is which (keep or toss). You may have heard the "rule" that you should touch a paper only once. You may even have tried — and failed — to practice that rule. It didn't work because you hadn't yet established your decision guidelines or built your decision muscle. The **TBR** category allows you to move FORWARD with organizing your papers while you're doing both.

Sort through this stack for your usual block of time to see how your decision muscle has grown and how your tools are working for you. Sort your **TBR** papers into the four categories from Step #22, **Let Go**, **Take Action**, **File It**, and **TBR**. Yes, you can put an item back in the **TBR** pile again. If you're not ready to decide to take action or to let go, then place it back in the box to revisit later. Over time and with practice the **TBR** pile will shrink, and the time it takes to decide what to do with a piece of paper will shorten.

Usually, you'd keep this category for last. You'd wait until all your paper piles had been sorted before going through this stack. However, I wanted you to practice working on the possibilities and opportunities that are ripening.

Continue to sort through your paper piles until you've gone through the stacks and what's left is either filed or in your TBR box(es). You'll continue sorting into the four categories from Step #22. Speaking of sorting, when's your next sorting session scheduled?

Sometimes facing opportunity is like staring at the knees of a giraffe.

Laurie Beth Jones

Is your decision muscle stronger?
_____

Was it easier to decide what to do?
_____

Once you've sorted through all the paper piles and you come back and start sorting the TBR box(es). You'll find that your decision muscle is much stronger. You'll be taking action on the priorities, letting go of a lot of possibilities, and keeping only the best opportunities to ripen in your **TBR** folder that you created in Step #23. You will probably always have a **TBR** folder because there will always be exciting ideas and wonderful opportunities that come along. You may not be ready to act on them. You may not be ready to decide what's next. But now you have a home for them. You have the **To Be Revisited** file. Use it and let those ideas ripen. Schedule your next paper sorting session if you haven't already.

SUMMARY

Tools:

- **TBR** Labeled Box
- **Let Go** containers (trash, recycle, shred, giveaway)
- **Take Action** box
- **File It** box

Time Estimate: _____ minutes (write in your set administration time) and save 15 minutes for clearing away the sorted piles.

Add Notes Here ↘

Grab your

- **TBR** box
- **Let Go** containers
- **Take Action** box
- **File It** box

Return to Step #22 and SORT into **Let Go, Take Action, File It,** and **To Be Revisited (TBR).**

Prevention — REFUSE

There are two commitments you must make to get and keep your papers in order so you can find what you need when you need it: 1) commit to putting time into maintaining your paper system (aka practice your organizing skills) and, 2) commit to preventing paper chaos.

In Steps #26 through #29, we will look at the four general ways you can *prevent* the paper chaos from starting again or getting worse.

The first is to REFUSE.

Whether they're brochures at the doctor's office, the free magazines at the grocery store, discount coupons, or handouts from the conference or home show event — refuse to take them. Unless it applies to an immediate project or issue, acknowledge that there is plenty of information out there on the web and at your local library. Refuse those fliers, handouts, etc. unless you've set aside time right now to read or act on them. You may need that phone number, but if it's lost in a pile of other papers, you won't find it and it's not useful. Say "no" to the freebies.

Simplicity is making the journey of this life with just baggage enough.

Charles Dudley Warner

Commit to saying 'no' to freebies for the next six days/weeks/months.

Build your "NO" muscle and say no to freebies.

SUMMARY

Tools: The word NO

Time: 15 minutes today to commit to saying "no" and 5 minutes before each event to remind yourself to say "no."

Add Notes Here ↘

Prevention — Reduce

The second way to prevent the paper chaos from starting again is to REDUCE the flow of paper coming into your home and the amount of paper you produce.

Stop the flow of junk mail into your home — congrats! You made a difference in Step #4. You will need to allow two to three months to see the full benefits of the reduction in unsolicited mail. Keep reducing the amount of incoming junk mail by updating your privacy preferences with companies as they send you their privacy policy each year. And follow through with your decision to toss immediately.

Stop the flow of catalogs into your home — congratulations, you started getting off the catalog mailing lists in Step #7. As another catalog comes in, take action. Let go of the idea that you'll look at it later. If you don't have time now, why do you think you'll have the time later? Get off the list and toss it.

Stop the flow of magazines — cheers again for taking action in Step #8. Buy a magazine when you have time to read it. Keep the subscriptions only to those magazines you read routinely. Let go of the rest. Reminder: if you take your magazines to the library, you'll still be able to read them when you do find the time.

Stop producing paper by reducing the number of emails and documents that you print. If you have a habit of printing emails or reports because they're easier to read, consider a few options. Increase the font size of your default email reader: Use the keyboard shortcut CTRL+PLUS SIGN to zoom in and make the text larger in your current window. Or read your email or document on an iPad or tablet with a higher resolution screen.

Stop printing multiple copies of anything. If your habit is to print a report or meeting minutes out immediately, but then forget where you put them in time for the meeting, consider two options: either don't print it until you go to the meeting, or make

You can never get enough of what you don't really need.

April Lane Benson

a notebook, file, or project container for the activity or organization. The notebook or project container creates a home to put it in and a place to find it when you need it.

One change that could help slow you down in printing out an item is to turn off your printer. Make it a conscious effort to print by turning it on before you hit the print button.

What habit or behavior will you focus on changing?

Take 15 minutes today and review where and how paper is coming into your life. Take another 15 minutes to answer the following questions:

- What habits do you have concerning paper and information that increase the amount of paper entering your home or office?

- Which one would you like to change?

- Which one would be the easiest?

- Which one would make the biggest difference?

Pick one habit or identify one behavior you'll change, and commit to reducing the amount of paper coming into your life.

SUMMARY

Tools:

- Your assessment of your paper flow
- Pen and paper to list possible changes
- Your commitment to making the change.

Time Estimate: 15 minutes to review where and how paper is coming into your life. Another 15 minutes to brainstorm one more way you can reduce paper flowing into your home, office and life.

> Review your incoming paper.
>
> Identify one change to make.
>
> Commit to that change.
>
> Reduce the flow.

Add Notes Here ⬇

Prevention — Reuse

Though we often think that reuse is one of the best ways to be environmentally green, when it comes to paper and the piles in your life, rethink reuse. It's your call on reusing paper, using the "other" side for notes and printing, but consider the amount of time you waste by searching for that note you wrote or figuring out which side of the paper you're currently using. Printing on the other side can be visually distracting. If there is not some clear indication of which side is current and important, you can waste time determining the important information.

If you do what you've always done, you will get what you've always gotten.

— Tony Robbins

Previously printed paper is harder on a printer then new, unused paper. It can cause paper jams, misfeeds, and the ink on the paper can increase wear and tear of the feed rollers and clean-up bars on laser printers. If you do reuse paper, then keep it flat and organized, no creases or folds, and ensure that each piece of paper is separated by fanning it out and loosening the stack before placing the used paper in the paper tray. Know which side should be up so that you don't print over previously printed material. That's a waste of expensive resources.

Does your reuse/scrap box often overflow and become a magnet for other disorganization? Set a limit of how much you'll keep to reuse. Choose ONE box and set the top edge as the limit. Anything more gets recycled.

How much will you keep to reuse?

_____

What will you reuse it for?

_____

I don't recommend reusing paper for notes that you want to keep or for task lists, but it can make good scratch paper. Cut the letter sized paper into four postcard-sized pieces. Then staple the stack together. Now you have a scratch pad that you can use to jot down temporary notes and then toss.

SUMMARY

Tools:

- Reuse/scrap box
- Recycle container
- Your decision on 'how much' and for what

Time Estimate: 15 minutes to consider whether reusing paper is truly an economical and environmentally friendly decision, given the cost of disorganization in your life.

Grab your

- Reuse/scrap box
- Recycle container

Commit to your limit of how much and for what use.

Add Notes Here ⬇

Prevention — Recycle

You don't need strength to let go of something. What you really need is understanding.

Guy Finley

The fourth way to prevent paper chaos is to plan your recycling and to get realistic about what you can do to help the environment. If you plan to recycle paper, answer these questions before the paper starts stacking up.

- Where will you take it or who will pick it up?

- What do they accept? Some may take envelopes; some might not. Some may take all colors; some won't. Know what can be recycled.

- When will you take it or when will it be picked up?

Will you set up an office recycle bin by the printer or desk and a larger recycle bin outside for storing until pickup day? Or just have the one in the office?

I recommend setting up your recycle station near where you do bills or by your printer. Anywhere that is easy to use. You might place it next to your trash and shredding bin. If you have to trek across the house to put it in the recycle bin, it's unlikely you'll routinely get it there. It's been piling up in the past, hasn't it? Make recycling as easy and as pain-free as possible.

If there is no easy way to recycle or there's just too much to deal with initially, consider putting it in the trash. I know, I know. You want to be environmentally conscious and not put more waste in the landfill. But until you can get a handle on your paper organization and keep the recycle manageable, consider the environmental cost of your stress and overwhelm. Think about how much energy those stacks and piles and bags of recycle are draining away from you. You can do more good if you have the energy and time to focus on making systemic changes rather than protecting the landfill from a couple of bags of trash. If you want to protect the environment, reduce the generation of items to be thrown away or recycled before it gets into your home.

Schedule your recycling. If there is curbside pickup, set a reminder to get it outside on time. If you have to take it, put it on your schedule now. Don't wait for *eventually*.

SUMMARY

Tools: Recycle box or container

Time Estimate: 30 minutes or less to determine when and where your recycled paper is going. 5 minutes to create a reminder or entry in your calendar of when the recycle goes. The time to get it there may vary from a few minutes to get it out on the curb to an hour to take it to the community recycle location.

Add Notes Here ↘

Grab your

- Recycle Container

Accept that you and your personal environment are as important as the larger

Final Storage Unit

Are the things around you helping you toward success—or are they holding you back?

W. Clement Stone

Now that you've built your decision muscle, established your guidelines, practiced your paper processing skills and tweaked your system, it's time to assess your final storage unit(s) and clear them out if necessary.

If you have filing drawers that have old papers and files that need to be cleared out, it's time to focus on clearing them out. Start with one drawer or a handful of files and return to Step #22. You'll sort the paper into **Let Go**, **Take Action**, **File It**, and **To Be Revisited** stacks. You'll use your **Keep or Toss Guide**, as well as your **Paper Questions**.

You will also assess your current file drawers if you have them:

- Do you need them? With your guidelines, how much space for filing do you need?

- Will your current filing drawers work for you? Do the drawers open smoothly? Do they open completely for easy access to all the files? Are there physical reasons they didn't work for you in the first place?

- Do you need to replace your current filing drawers?

When and if you choose to get filing drawers, go top of the line for quality hardware. I only recommend HON. After 12 years in a tropical environment, the hardware, slides, etc. on my HON filing drawers were still operating smoothly and easily. These are not cheap, but they will save you time and energy. And ultimately, you'll save money because your filing tool works and continues to keep working for you. You won't have to buy a replacement.

Step #30 to Organize Your Paper | 97

SUMMARY

Tools: Sorting bins/containers with labels as needed

- **Trash** can
- **Recycle** bin for paper
- **Shred** box — either to shred or to take to a shredding site
- Box for **Giveaway** — labeled
- Box for **Take Action Not Now** — labeled
- Tray or folder or target area for **Take Action Now** (after sorting session is completed)
- Box for **File It** — labeled
- Box for **TBR** — labeled
- Sticky notes
- Marker (for writing the labels)
- A timer

Time Estimate: _____ minutes (write in your set administration time) + 15 minutes for clearing away the sorted piles. 5 minutes to schedule your next paper sorting session.

Grab your containers:

- ❑ Trash
- ❑ Recycle
- ❑ Shred
- ❑ Giveaway
- ❑ Action – **Now**
- ❑ Action – **Not Now**
- ❑ File
- ❑ **TBR**

SORT

Use sticky notes to provide reminders of who, where, what, when

Add Notes Here ↘

Keep Going

The flow of paper into your life and home has been slowed by your efforts in the last 30 steps; however, it won't stop it altogether. You've created guidelines, habits, homes, and strategies. Now you need to rinse-repeat until your old paper piles have been cleared and your current paper is managed well.

There are going to be times when life turns your attention away from your efforts to manage the paper. The progress you've made may be put on hold. The systems you've built suddenly don't work as smoothly as they did before. That's natural. That's normal. But congratulations, the time it will take you to get back into handling your papers quickly and efficiently will be less than you fear and certainly less than it took when you started.

The goal of this step is for you to commit to yourself that you will keep going. Paper management is not a one and done activity. Dealing with the paper that comes into your life is and will continue to be an ongoing event. Information will keep flowing into our lives, and for now, paper is still the primary format many of us choose for that information. Commit to processing your mail routinely. Commit to making decisions on the paper that you do allow in. Schedule your next paper sorting session!

Sometimes it's easier to keep a commitment to keep going with someone else. Let your paperwork partners know — let me know — that you're committed to taking these steps. Email me at simplify@dhucks.com or connect with me on Facebook @DHUCKSinaRow.

Success is not measured by what you accomplish, but by the opposition you have encountered, and the courage with which you have maintained the struggle against overwhelming odds.

Orison Swett Marden

When is your next paper sorting session?

_____

SUMMARY

Tools: your paper partners, me, or a pen & notepad to record your commitment to keep going.

Time Estimate: 15 minutes or less

Add Notes Here ↘

Commit to Keep Going

Commit to continuing to take these small steps

Thank Someone

Congratulations, you did it! You took 31 small steps toward organizing your paper. Take some time to thank someone who helped you with your journey (especially yourself).

As for me, I would like to thank my newsletter readers. If it hadn't been for you I wouldn't have written some of these chapters initially as articles. If I hadn't written the articles first, I wouldn't have made the time to build these steps into a book. Thank you for being there to read, respond, and request. You've made all the difference. Thank you, Readers!

Shawndra

Gratitude makes sense of our past, brings peace for today, and creates a vision for tomorrow.

Melody Beattie

Appendix A — Glossary

Term	Definition
Accountability partner	Someone who helps you stick to what you say you'll do. The best accountability partner is one who is non-judgmental but is willing to ask "why not?" when you don't follow through with what you committed to doing.
Action Items folder	This is the home for any piece of paper you need to take action on once you've processed it and have decided that you still need to keep it. If the information doesn't fit in your calendar or on your task list, keep the paper and place it here.
Action tools	The tools that you use to take action on your paper. Your calendar (Step #19) and to-do or task list (Step #20)
Catalog Home	Refer to **Magazine Home** for more details. A separate home for catalogs is necessary only when you have determined that you need more catalogs than will fit in the **Magazine Home**.
Chronic Disorganization	Chronic disorganization is having a past history of disorganization in which self-help efforts to change have failed, an undermining of current quality of life due to disorganization, and the expectation of future disorganization. Definition from the Institute for Challenging Disorganization (www.challengingdisorganization.org/content/what-definition-chronic-disorganization)
Chunk of Time	A small period of time in which you work. This time period is small enough to keep you willing to organize, but large enough that you can make progress. It's intended to break up a larger block of time and help you refocus on your original goal or intention. 15 minutes is a natural chunk of time, but 20, 23, and 30 minutes are also common. However, 5, 7, and 10 minutes can also be used if that's all the time you have.

Term	Definition
CPO-CD®	Certified Professional Organizer in Chronic Disorganization. Certified from the Institute for Challenging Disorganization. The CPO-CD® certified individual is a professional organizer who has been educated in depth on the issues of chronic disorganization.
DMA	Data & Marketing Association. Previously known as Direct Marketing Association.
eMPS	Email Preference Service sponsored by Data & Marketing Association (DMA) that allows you to remove your email from national DMA lists.
File categories	Broad categories that help you find the piece of paper you're looking for. Categories vary by individual. See Step #21.
File It	This is one of the four categories that you will sort your stacks of paper into. Those papers that you need to store or archive (refer to your **Keep or Toss Guide**) will go into the **File It** box. You can then focus on filing the papers in another session.
Final storage unit	The initial and secondary paper storage units may be your final storage units. However, if you have file drawers or want file drawers, Step #30 addresses clearing old file drawers or purchasing new ones.
Guidelines	Rules that determine what you will do and when you will do it. You set these rules or guidelines on what to do with a specific piece of paper the first time. Then all subsequent decisions on similar paper are easier. Decide once, take action repeatedly with minimal effort and energy.
Home	An established location that an item or piece of paper returns to after being used. This is also the location that you go to when you want the item or piece of paper.

Term	Definition
ICD	Institute for Challenging Disorganization (www.challengingdisorganization.com)
Initial paper storage unit	A file box that holds the various folders you will create or have created during these 31 Small Steps. The initial storage unit can be a temporary paper storage unit until you clear out your current file drawers or purchase a set of file drawers. You may also find that this storage unit may be sufficient for your needs once you've developed your **Keep or Toss Guide** in Step #14.
Keep Going	IMPORTANT! Make this your motto when you feel overwhelmed and ready to quit because you have too much paper and too many piles. Keep going. A day at a time. One small step at a time. Keep going!
Keep or Toss Guide	Rules or guidelines that you establish to help you decide whether a piece of paper needs to be kept or when it can be tossed. See Step #14.
Let Go	This is one of the four categories that you will sort your stacks of paper into. Paper that goes into this category will be shredded or destroyed, recycled, placed in the trash, or given away.
Magazine Home	A container holding magazines or other reading material to be read. Consider this as your target or drop zone for anything you've decided to read. It can include catalogs and books. Preferred: open box or basket that is large enough for a limited number of magazines to fit. If I give you a specific number of magazines, such as 10, you may ask, "what about 12?" Think fewer than you want but not so few that you refuse to use the **Magazine Home**. Keep it small enough to prevent junk or non-reading items from being tossed in. Location: where you're most likely to read.

Term	Definition
Mail Home	A container holding incoming mail or other paperwork to be processed. Consider this as your target or drop zone for mail. Preferred: open box or basket that is large enough for a large envelope but small enough to prevent junk or non-paper items from being tossed in.
Maintenance	Required action to keep your system, space, and life organized. Consider reframing the word maintenance as *practice* using organizational skills.
Mobile processing center or toolkit	A tool for processing your incoming mail. It consists of a box or container with any tools you use to open mail, pay bills, send mail, or otherwise process paper. See Step #10 for a list of possible tools to include.
Monthly folders	Twelve hanging folders that are labeled **January** through **December** and placed in the initial paper storage unit. These twelve **Monthly** folders are for paper (bills, statements, etc.) that you do not need to retain longer than a year. Items are filed by the month you process them rather than by vendor or topic. Maintenance of the files has been built in because as you move to the next month, you'll remove last year's paper to open up the space for this year's.
NAID	National Association for Information Destruction (www.naidonline.org)
NAPO	National Association of Organizers (www.napo.net)
Now and **Not Now**	Timeframes for taking action. There are other timeframes that you can use such as Today, This Week, This Month, Next Month. Starting with **Now** and **Not Now** can help you simplify the sorting and listing of actions items. **Now** is today and **Not Now** is later.

Term	Definition
OCR	Optical Character Recognition. OCR allows the content within a PDF to be searched.
Organization	Finding what you want when you want it. Organization looks different for each person. It's based on their needs, their challenges, and their goals.
Paper maintenance system	The whole process from the moment mail enters your life to when it leaves. The paper maintenance system includes your tools, strategies, habits, and decisions. Tools such as the **Mail Home**, your mobile processing center/toolkit, decision guidelines, timer, etc. Strategies such as setting guidelines, using **Monthly** folders instead of vendor or topic folders, chunking your work time to remind you to refocus if you're distracted, etc. Habits such as using a timer, doing bills or processing your paper on a set day of the month, dropping your bill statements into the Monthly folder instead of leaving it on the corner of the table, etc. Decisions such as how long you will keep non-tax related bills instead of piling them up indefinitely, committing to 15 minutes a day instead of putting it off again, letting go of the *someday maybe* items, or making those *someday maybe* items a priority today, etc.
Paper Questions	Six questions to ask yourself when faced with paper you don't have a guideline for already. See Step #14.
Paperless	No such thing as paper free. However, going with less paper (paperLESS) is possible. Is it right for you? That depends. Check out Step #18 and start there.

Term	Definition
Paperwork Party™	A two-hour session working on paperwork, bills, email, filing, organizing an office, clearing a space, or sorting while others are doing the same. Paperwork Party™ is trademarked by Shawndra Holmberg and Dhucks.
PDF	Common file format. PDF stands for Portable Document Format.
Practice	"Practice makes improvement." Quote from Keith Harrell
Prevention	It is better to stop paper entering your life than it is to deal with the paper piling up.
Professional Organizer	A trained expert in establishing systems, transferring skills, and offering tools and strategies. Professional Organizers may specialize in certain areas such as space management, time management, Attention-Deficit / Hyperactivity Disorder, etc. Ask questions and choose someone who fits your needs.
Read-by Date	A date that you commit to reading a specific magazine, brochure, book, or catalog. Seriously, if you haven't gotten to that magazine in six months, let it go. More are probably coming in, so read it or let it go.
Recycle	Don't bury your home in paper waiting for the recycling in your community to catch up to your desire to save the environment. Be realistic.
Reduce	Stop the flow of mail into your life. Stop the flow of reading material. Stop printing and creating more paper.
Refuse	Say NO! to paper coming into your life unless you have a plan to handle it.

Term	Definition
Reuse	Reuse carefully. Don't keep excessive amounts of used paper around. Keep only what you can reasonably use.
Rule of 6	Information is old after 6 editions. Information in a daily newspaper is old after 6 days. A monthly magazine is old after 6 months. Let go of anything older than 6.
Secondary storage unit	This storage unit will contain your various file categories if the initial paper storage unit is too small. It may also contain your Tax Archives and other file categories.
Shredding guidelines	Rules or guidelines that you establish to help you decide what needs to be shredded and what doesn't. You also decide who will destroy the information. If you will be doing the shredding, you decide when you will do it. See Step #13.
Someday	A period of time that never arrives.
Sorting Station	An area for sorting your paper piles that includes: a trash can, recycle container, your shredding box, a container to hold the giveaways, and containers for your **TBR**, **File It**, **Take Action**, and other tools you need.
Take Action box	This is one of the four categories that you will sort your stacks of paper into. Papers that go into this sorting category are ones that you need to do something with (other than file or toss). These papers might include tasks to do or projects to work on.
Take Action tool	The tools that you use to take action on your paper: your calendar (Step #19) and to-do or task list (Step #20).
Task List	Previously known as a to-do list. A tool to help you empty your brain of reminders. It is not in charge of your day — you are. Think could-do, or possible action list. You get to decide the priority.

Term	Definition
Tax Archives	Ten extra-capacity hanging folders labeled 0 - 9 that hold your tax archives. The folder labeled 0 can hold 2010 or 2020. "6" can hold 2006, 2016, or 2026. "9" can hold 2009, 2019, or 2029. If you determined that you need to keep your tax files for a shorter or longer period, this system may not work for you. The 10 folders are intended to make maintenance and destruction more manageable, not establish how long you should keep your tax information.
Taxes folder	One hanging folder placed in the initial paper storage unit that will hold the current year's tax documents. Documents such as receipts, statements, etc.
TBR	See **To Be Revisited**
Timer	An essential tool for refocusing on what you intended to do, rather than what drew your attention away. Basic requirements are an auditory or vibrational indication at the end of your chunk of time to remind you, "Hey! Get back to what you said you wanted to do right now! ☺"
To Be Revisited (TBR)	This is one of the four categories that you will sort your stacks of paper into. This category is used for paper and items that you're not sure you want to keep, but you're not ready to let go. If you answer "I don't know," "I don't have a clue," or "I'm not sure" to the question of do you need it or do you want it, then this is the category to put it in for now. The **To Be Revisited (TBR)** pile, box, or file is a tool to keep you sorting, deciding, and moving forward by setting the piece of paper aside for now. It can also be thought of as ripening.

Term	Definition
To File folder	One hanging folder placed in the initial paper storage unit that will hold any papers that you choose to file *later*. Once you've created the files in Step #21, this folder should only need to be used when you don't already have a file established for a piece of paper. This is a temporary holding spot for paper awaiting a permanent home folder.
To-Do list	A tool to help you empty your brain of reminders. It is not in charge of your day — you are. Think could-do, task, or action list. You get to decide the priority. Use **Task List** instead.
Toss	Broad term that includes placing an item in the trash, recycling, shredding, or giving it away.

Appendix B — Shopping List

Before Starting

- ☐ **Timer**
  - Options: www.dhucks.com/shoppinglist-31smallsteps-paper
  - Check Out: The Time Timer® (www.timetimer.com)

Step #1

- ☐ **Additional Task Lighting** if needed

Step #3

- ☐ **Basket or Container** for mail
  - Options: www.dhucks.com/shoppinglist-31smallsteps-paper

Step #5

- ☐ **Basket or Container** for magazines and reading material
  - Options: www.dhucks.com/shoppinglist-31smallsteps-paper

Step #10

- ☐ **Project Case or Container** to hold your mail processing tools
  - Options: www.dhucks.com/shoppinglist-31smallsteps-paper
  - Check Out: IRIS Portable Project Case

Step #11

- ☐ **File Box** as your initial paper storage unit
  - Options: www.dhucks.com/shoppinglist-31smallsteps-paper
  - Check Out: IRIS Portable WEATHERTIGHT File Box

Step #12

- ☐ **Hanging File Folders** (box of 25, you'll use them in later steps also)
- ☐ **Hanging File Folder Tabs – CLEAR**
  - Options: www.dhucks.com/shoppinglist-31smallsteps-paper

Step #13

- ☐ **Shredder or Shredding Company**
  - Options: www.dhucks.com/shoppinglist-31smallsteps-paper

Step #19

- ☐ **Calendar** use what you have and tweak it first
  - Options: www.dhucks.com/shoppinglist-31smallsteps-paper

Step #20
- ❏ **Lists**
    - Options: www.dhucks.com/shoppinglist-31smallsteps-paper

Step #21
- ❏ **Hanging File Folders** (~7, if you don't have them already)
- ❏ **Extra Capacity Hanging File Folders** (10)
- ❏ **Hanging File Folder Tabs – CLEAR**
- ❏ **File Storage Box** as your second paper storage unit if needed
    - Options: www.dhucks.com/shoppinglist-31smallsteps-paper
    - Check Out: IRIS 32 Quart WEATHERTIGHT Storage Box

Step #23
- ❏ **Hanging File Folders** (2, if you don't have them already)
- ❏ **Hanging File Folder Tabs - CLEAR**
    - Options: www.dhucks.com/shoppinglist-31smallsteps-paper

Step #30
- ❏ **File drawers** (only if you need and want them)
    - Options: www.dhucks.com/shoppinglist-31smallsteps-paper
    - Check Out: HON 2-Drawer Full-Suspension Letter File

Appendix C — Organizing Zones

Not everything you keep can occupy the same space, so identifying storage and organizing zones for your paper is important.

Think

(Red)   (Yellow)   (Blue)

Use Hot Zones for paper, information, and related tools that you access daily or weekly. These items are placed closest to the area where you do your paper activity, such as mail process, bill paying, bookkeeping, writing, project planning, etc.

The intent is to keep these items easy to access and within arm's reach. Look at the drawers, shelves, walls, and flat surfaces around you. Areas that you can reach without getting out of your seat are **HOT ZONES**. They are prime real estate; keep them clear of clutter and keep the space free for the things you use most often. This zone could be used for your cell phone, planner, motivational reminders, and, of course, your computer, as well as reference books, notebooks, and routinely accessed files.

Hot zones aren't just in your office space. Think of the hot zones near the doors you enter and exit your home or your office. Are there opportunities to place furniture, hooks, baskets, or other organizing tools nearby to make these hot zones usable?

Use Warm Zones for those items that you only access a couple of times a month or year. You can put a bit of an effort into locating these things so they don't have to be taking up your prime real estate. You can stand up and stretch to reach the box on the top shelf to get the specialty paper you only use for holiday letters. You can kneel to look into that bottom file drawer to pull out your insurance file folder. You can walk across the room to grab a reference notebook off the bookcase. Remember to put the items back when you're done.

The intent is to keep these items available but not within arm's reach. Look at the drawers, bookshelves, walls, and flat surfaces around you. Identify areas that you can access with a minimum amount of effort but aren't in your hot zones. These are your **WARM ZONES**. These zones can be used for reference material, specialty items, and equipment you use sporadically.

Use Cold Zones for archives, the information that you need to keep but won't access very often, if ever (taxes, important papers). Getting to these files can require more effort. Archives and cold files don't necessarily have to be in the same room necessarily. Important papers might be in a fire safe, safety deposit box at your bank, or any secure location you've chosen. Tax files can be in a box or file drawer at the back of a storage closet. It's likely you're only going to access this one time a year. Of course, your current tax file, where you drop your receipts and statements in often, should be in your Hot Zone.

The intent is to keep these items but to keep them out of your everyday space. Look at high spots (for lightweight items — don't put heavy boxes over your head), low areas, far corners, under other Warm Zone boxes, and options in other rooms. These will be your **COLD ZONES**.

Organizing Zones

You can use the idea of Hot, Warm, and Cold zones for the various activities in your space. Think of *what* you do and *where*. Then stage your tools and supplies according to the zones. You can also apply organizing zones to your garage, bedroom, kitchen, and clothes.

Appendix D — Special Categories

BOOKS

If you are finding it hard to open up the space and let go of some of your books, take time to revisit the book (not just the memories) and determine if you still need the book physically on your bookshelf. Maybe you don't. And, just maybe, the book is lonely and needs to be held by someone new, by someone who hasn't yet discovered the joys within as you have.

OWNER'S MANUALS:

You could go paperless and toss them if you've confirmed they are available on-line. You could also download the PDF and keep an electronic file. But if you've decided to keep the paper copies of your owner's manuals, I suggest you keep them in the room where the equipment is. Place a wall file in a cabinet or closet and drop your manuals in it.

PHOTOS:

If you've been talking about someday putting all your photos into albums (or scanning), take your first step towards that goal today by getting your photos into one place. I strongly recommend using photo boxes that are archive quality to store your photos in — for now. Don't organize them, just put all the photos you come across into your boxes — for now. You can toss out duplicates and out-of-focus shots, but no sorting by date, subject, or event. The idea is to get them safely stored until you're ready to move to the next step.

If you're wondering what to do with your photo albums, display them on a shelf so you can enjoy them easily or give them to friends or family members to enjoy. You can also have them scanned and uploaded to the cloud or put on a disc. Want help organizing your photos? Go to www.appo.org, Association of Personal Photo Organizers (APPO), to find a trained photo organizer near you.

RECIPES:

Get rid of the ones you don't use. If you have a pile of recipes you'd like to try, make a point of trying a new recipe each week. If you don't use them, but don't want to lose them because they are old family recipes, go electronic. You could create a recipe folder on your computer and add a recipe each week. If you have a scanner, scan it in. Or even delegate — pay a student to type it.

If it's important enough to keep, it's important enough to use. Check out two ways to organize your recipes "as is." Instead of waiting for *someday* to organize your recipes perfectly, organize them as-is and use them today.

Build a recipe notebook or use an expanding file folder. Examples of the suggested materials can be found at pinterest.com/shawndraholmber/31-recipes.

RECIPE NOTEBOOK:

Buy a notebook that is intended to be used with sheet protectors and dividers. It's extra wide.

Use sheet protectors for recipes as-is. I suggest Snap-In protectors so that you don't have to open the rings to move the recipes, but any sheet protector will do. Top-loading is best. Just drop your recipe in, whether it's cut from a magazine, printed from the web or written on a recipe card.

Use tabbed dividers that are made to be used with sheet protectors. Otherwise the tabs will disappear.

RECIPE FILES:

Use an expanding file folder to sort your recipes into categories. No additional preparation needed. The one main drawback to using a file folder is that you may have to pull all the recipes out of a section to find the one you want, but it certainly would be less time than going through a stack of unsorted recipes. You can even create a category TO TRY. Grab one once a week or once a month. Then drop it in the appropriate category or toss it when you're done.

WARRANTIES:

Where are your owner's manuals? Put them there. And make sure your receipts are attached as well. Some companies are now making specific suggestions on where you should keep your warranties. For example, I was directed to place the warranty information for my new mattress between the box springs and the mattress. I have a hat (yes, a hat with a warranty) that suggests placing the warranty information in the left-hand side of my sock drawer. If I call and can't remember where I put it, they know where to direct me (if I followed their suggestion).

Appendix E — Resources

Website resources listed in this book

- Amazon, www.amazon.com
- Association of Personal Photo Organizers (APPO), www.appo.org
- CatalogChoice, www.CatalogChoice.org
- Data & Marketing Association, www.DMAchoice.org
- DocumentSnap Solutions, www.documentsnap.com
- Email Preference Service (eMPS), www.ims-dm.com/cgi/optoutemps.php
- Institute for Challenging Disorganization (ICD), www.challengingdisorganization.com
- IRS, *How long should I keep records?*, www.irs.gov/businesses/small-businesses-self-employed/how-long-should-i-keep-records
- **Keep or Toss Guide** development course, www.hyh.thinkific.com/courses/building-your-keep-or-toss-guide
- National Association for Information Destruction (NAID), directory.naidonline.org
- National Association of Professional Organizers (NAPO), www.napo.net
- The Time Timer, www.timetimer.com
- OptOutPrescreen.com, www.OptOutPrescreen.com
- Paperwork Party™, www.dhucks.com/paperwork-party
- Removing or deleting yourself from the internet
    - www.cnet.com/how-to/remove-delete-yourself-from-the-internet
    - www.zdnet.com/article/how-to-remove-yourself-from-people-search-websites

- Unroll.me, www.unroll.me
- Virtual Organizer, www.virtualorganizers.com

Resources located on the Dhucks.com website

- Downloads and links mentioned in this book, www.dhucks.com/resources31smallsteps-paper
- Blog, www.dhucks.com/blog
- Need help with commitment? Join my Paperwork Party™. www.dhucks.com/paperwork-party

Additional Dhucks' resources

- Pinterest page, www.pinterest.com/shawndraholmber
- Dhucks' **Keep or Toss Guide** development course, www.hyh.thinkific.com/courses/building-your-keep-or-toss-guide
- Dhucks' 31 Small Steps to Organize Your Paper online course, www.hyh.thinkific.com/courses/31-small-steps-to-organize-your-paper

so, who's this shawndra person, anyway?

Shawndra Holmberg has been organizing longer than the eleven years she's been running her business, **Dhucks**. She believes in the power that an organized space, schedule, and life have on our creative spirit. She knows there's not one right way to get organized, and she's trained to make your organization work for you. She is a Certified Professional Organizer in Chronic Disorganization (CPO-CD®) and is focused on being your personal trainer for productivity, a mentor for your goals, and a motivational force for your creativity.

Shawndra considers herself a lousy tourist as she usually spends her vacations enjoying a good book (reading one or writing one) and drinking coffee on her lanai, deck, porch, or sunroom. That's why she prefers to live and work in interesting locales. She worked on Johnston Island (approximately 850 miles southwest of Hawai'i), spent a year at the South Pole, Antarctica, and then thawed out in Hawai'i. She is currently enjoying the people and scenery of Western Pennsylvania as she organizes and coaches writers and others who are reaching for their dream. She is located in Pennsylvania but works virtually everywhere.

and what's this about a dhuck?

Dhucks are fun, playful and cute. What better mascot for organizing or *getting your dhucks in a row*. Shawndra has had a life-long interest in getting her dhucks in a row, whether it's getting organized, losing weight, reaching for a dream, or finding the joy in each day. Join the fun and *get your dhucks in a row*.

Made in the USA
Middletown, DE
02 September 2020